Great Expectations

by Charles Dickens

Peter Morrisson

Series Editors:
Sue Bennett and Dave Stockwin

HODDER
EDUCATION
AN HACHETTE UK COMPANY

The publisher would like to thank the following for permission to reproduce copyright material:

Photo credits:

p. 8 The Keasbury-Gordon Photograph Archive/Alamy; **p. 17, 27** Moviestore collection Ltd/Alamy; **p. 18** The Granger Collection/TopFoto; **pp. 37, 62** Pictorial Press Ltd/Alamy; **p. 39** AF archive/Alamy; **p. 49** ITV/ Rex Features

Although every effort has been made to ensure that website addresses are correct at time of going to press, Hodder Education cannot be held responsible for the content of any website mentioned. It is sometimes possible to find a relocated web page by typing in the address of the home page for a website in the URL window of your browser.

Orders: please contact Bookpoint Ltd, 130 Park Drive, Milton Park, Abingdon, Oxon OX14 4SB. Telephone: (44) 01235 827720. Fax: (44) 01235 400454. Lines are open 9.00–17.00, Monday to Saturday, with a 24-hour message answering service. Visit our website at www.hoddereducation.co.uk

© Peter Morrison 2016

First published in 2016 by

Hodder Education

An Hachette UK Company,

Carmelite House, 50 Victoria Embankment

London EC4Y 0LS

Impression number	5	4	3	2	1
Year	2020	2019	2018	2017	2016

Cover photo Veneratio/Fotolia

Typeset in Bliss Light 11/13 by Integra Software Services Pvt. Ltd., Pondicherry, India

Printed in Italy

A catalogue record for this title is available from the British Library.

ISBN 9781471853593

Contents

Getting the most from this guide

This guide is designed to help you raise your achievement in your examination response for *Great Expectations*. It is intended for you to use throughout your GCSE English literature course: it will help you when you are studying the novel for the first time and also during your revision.

The following features have been used throughout this guide to help you focus your understanding of the novel.

Target your thinking

A list of **introductory questions** labelled by Assessment Objective is provided at the beginning of each chapter to give you a breakdown of the material covered. They target your thinking in order to help you work more efficiently by focusing on the key messages.

Build critical skills

These boxes offer an opportunity to consider some **more challenging questions**. They are designed to encourage deeper thinking, analysis and exploratory thought. Building and practising critical skills in this way will give you a real advantage in the examination.

GRADE *FOCUS*

It is possible to know a novel well and yet still underachieve in the examination if you are unsure what the examiners are looking for. The **GRADE FOCUS** boxes give a clear explanation of **how you may be assessed**, with an emphasis on the criteria for gaining a Grade 5 and a Grade 8.

REVIEW YOUR LEARNING

At the end of each chapter you will find this section to **test your knowledge**: a series of short specific questions to ensure you have understood and absorbed the key messages of the section. Answers to the 'Review your learning' questions are provided in the final section of the guide (p.100).

GRADE *BOOSTER*

Read and remember these pieces of helpful **grade-boosting advice**. They provide top tips from experienced teachers and examiners who can advise you on what to do, as well as what not to do, in order to maximise your chances of success in the examination.

Key quotation

'I love her, I love her, I love her!'
(Chapter 29, p.243)

Key quotations are highlighted for you, so that if you wish you may use them as **supporting evidence** in your examination answers. All the page references provided are from the Penguin Classics edition of the text. For each page reference, a chapter reference has also been given in case you are using a different edition.

Further quotations grouped by characterisation, key moments and theme can be found in the 'Top quotations' section on p.93.

Introduction

Studying the text

You may find it useful to read sections of this guide when you need them, rather than reading it from start to finish. For example, the section on Context can be read before you read the novel itself, since it offers an explanation of relevant historical, cultural and literary background to the text. In Context you will find information about aspects of Dickens' life and times that influenced his writing, the particular issues with which Dickens was concerned, and where the novel stands in terms of the literary tradition to which it belongs.

As you work through the novel, you may find it helpful to read the relevant plot and structure sections before or after reading a particular chapter. As well as a summary of events there is also commentary, so that you are aware of both key events and features in each of the chapters. The sections on characterisation, themes, and language, style and analysis will help to develop your thinking further, in preparation for written responses on particular aspects of the text.

Many students also enjoy the experience of being able to bring something extra to their classroom lessons in order to be 'a step ahead of the game'. Alternatively, you may have missed a classroom session or feel that you need a clearer explanation, and the guide can help you with this too.

An initial reading of the section on 'Assessment Objectives and skills' will enable you to make really effective notes in preparation for assessments. The Assessment Objectives are what examination boards base their mark schemes on. In this section the AOs are broken down and clearly explained.

Revising the text

Whether you study the novel in a block of time close to the exam or much earlier in your GCSE course, you will need to revise thoroughly if you are to achieve the very best grade that you can.

You should first remind yourself of what happens in the novel, and for this the chapter on 'Plot and structure' might be returned to in the first instance. You might then look at the 'Assessment Objectives and skills' section to ensure that you understand what the examiners are looking for in general.

'Tackling the examination questions' then gives you useful information on question format, depending on which examination board specification you are following, as well as advice on the examination format, and practical considerations such as the time available for the question and the assessment objectives that apply to it. Advice is also supplied on how to approach the question, writing a quick plan, and 'working with' the text, since all of the examination boards use an extract-based question for *Great Expectations*.

Focused advice on how you might improve your grade follows, and you need to read this section carefully.

You will also find examples of exam-style responses in the 'Sample essays' section, with an examiner's comments in the margins so that you can see clearly how to move towards a Grade 5 and how then to move from a Grade 5 to a Grade 8.

Now that all GCSE literature examinations are 'closed book', the 'Top quotations' section will be an invaluable aid, in that it offers you the opportunity to learn short quotations to support points about character and themes, as well as being a revision aid that identifies the top ten key moments in the novel.

When writing about the novel, use this guide as a springboard to develop your own ideas. Remember: the examiners are not looking for set responses. You should not read this guide in order to memorise chunks of it, ready to regurgitate in the exam. Identical answers are dull. The examiners hope to reward you for perceptive thought, individual appreciation and varying interpretations. They want to sense that you have engaged with the themes and ideas in the novel, have explored Dickens' methods with an awareness of the context in which he wrote and have enjoyed this part of your literature course.

There are a number of film and TV versions of *Great Expectations*, ranging from the classic 1946 black-and-white film directed by David Lean, to the 2011 TV serialisation starring Douglas Booth, Ray Winstone and Gillian Anderson, and the 2012 Mike Newell film with Ben Lloyd-Hughes, Holliday Grainger and Helena Bonham Carter. You will find interesting interpretations of and variations from the text in all of these but, of course, they should never be seen as a substitute for the text itself.

Context

Target your thinking

- What is meant by 'context'? (**AO3**)
- How did Charles Dickens' life influence his writing? (**AO3**)
- To what extent are historical events an influence on *Great Expectations*? (**AO3**)
- Is the novel still relevant to modern readers? (**AO3**)

The 'context' of a novel means the circumstances in which it was written – the social, historical and literary factors that influenced what the author wrote. All literature is influenced by the life experiences of the author and these in turn are shaped by the world in which he/she lived. Therefore, in order to truly understand *Great Expectations* (1860–61), it is necessary to have some understanding of both Dickens' life and Dickens' world.

Charles Dickens' life

Early years

▲ Charles Dickens

Charles Dickens was born in Portsmouth on 7 February 1812. His father, John Dickens, was a clerk in the Naval Pay Office and his mother, Elizabeth, had been a housekeeper to the wealthy Lord Crewe. In 1817, the family relocated to Chatham in Kent, where they lived until 1822. The nearby city of Rochester later became the model for Pip's home town in *Great Expectations*, from which Pip takes the coach to and from London. In 1821, while living at Chatham, Dickens attended a local school run by a Baptist minister, where he proved to be a most able pupil.

In 1822, the family again relocated, this time to the great metropolis of London. The shock of this move to the young Charles may well be reflected in Pip's account of his first encounter with the city, in which he is overwhelmed by the 'immensity of London' (Chapter 20, p.163). In 1824, John Dickens fell into debt and, apart from Charles, who began working at Warren's Blacking Factory (see below), the entire family was incarcerated in the Marshalsea Debtors' Prison in London. This dark period of Charles Dickens' young life influenced a number of his later novels and clearly illustrates how a writer's art is influenced by personal experience.

The impact of debt

Debt, a recurring theme

The theme of debt occurs in *David Copperfield* (1849–50). In this novel, Mr Micawber, modelled on John Dickens, is a kindly but financially incompetent man who struggles painfully to make his income cover his expenses. Similarly, *Little Dorrit* (1855–57) features a heroine, Amy Dorrit, whose father has spent many years imprisoned in the Marshalsea Debtors' Prison.

Great Expectations (1860–61) also explores the tragic potential of debt. On arriving in London, Pip describes being shown 'the Debtors' Door, out of which culprits came to be hanged' (Chapter 20, p.166). Debt also becomes a major feature in Pip's own life. He escapes imprisonment only because of the generosity of Joe, who selflessly clears all his bills (Chapter 57).

After three months of being incarcerated in the Marshalsea, John Dickens managed to liberate himself and his family as a result of a fortunately timed inheritance.

The boot-blacking factory

During the period of the family's incarceration, a relative of Elizabeth Dickens tried to assist the family by arranging for young Charles to begin work in Warren's boot-blacking business. Just as he reached twelve, this sensitive and highly intelligent boy had to forgo his education in order to begin monotonous days spent packaging bottles of shoe polish for six shillings a week.

> **GRADE** *BOOSTER*
>
> The examiner will not be impressed if you turn your literature essay on *Great Expectations* into a potted biography of the life and times of Charles Dickens. Only use this biographical information if you can show its relevance to the examination question and to events, characters or themes in the actual novel.

Although Dickens had to endure this menial occupation for only a matter of months, it left an indelible impression on his mind. As with debt, child exploitation became a major theme in his novels. *Oliver Twist* (1837–39) deals with the ruthless mistreatment of children throughout Victorian society – from corrupt workhouses, to heartless employers, to an insensitive and uncaring legal system. *David Copperfield* (1849–50), Dickens' most autobiographical novel, touches closely on his own personal experience at Warren's. Aged ten, David Copperfield is withdrawn from school by his cruel stepfather, Mr Murdstone, and sent to labour in a wine-bottling factory. David works six days a week, from 7:00 a.m. to 8:00 p.m., for six shillings a week.

Great Expectations also pursues this theme. Like the young Charles Dickens, the youthful Pip hankers after an education and a higher social status than that afforded him as a blacksmith's apprentice. It is clear, however, that the mature Pip who narrates the novel admires Joe Gargery's thrift and industry.

Education and social advancement

Not long after his family's release from prison, Dickens was removed from his detested employment. In 1825 he resumed his schooling, attending Wellington House Academy in London as a day pupil. In 1827, at the age of 15, he began work as a clerk in an attorney's office. Just 18 months later, he set out as a freelance reporter in the court of Doctors' Commons.

His various experiences of the law also later influenced Dickens' writing. The corruption, insensitivity or incompetence of the legal profession became another major focus in his novels. Dickens' greatest indictment of the legal system occurs in *Bleak House* (1852–53), in which the self-serving legal profession slowly grinds down the financial resources and spiritual wellbeing of all those who pursue a disputed will. For an analysis of Dickens' treatment of the law in *Great Expectations* (see pp. 48–50 of this guide).

Dickens was able to advance his own position in life to that of a freelance reporter because he had received an education as a child and because he had sufficient ambition to teach himself shorthand. By 1834, he had risen still further and joined the staff of the *Morning Chronicle*. In 1836, he began to publish, in serialised form, his first novel, *The Pickwick Papers*. *Pickwick* won him fame and success and firmly established his career as a novelist by the age of just 25. It is no wonder, therefore, that education is such an important theme in so many of Dickens' novels.

Falling in love

In 1836 Dickens married Catherine Hogarth; they would have ten children. In 1857, Dickens met and fell in love with a young actress called Ellen Ternan. The following year, he separated from Catherine, his wife of 22 years. In 1860, he sold his London home and moved to Gad's Hill Place, a large mansion he had purchased in 1856 on the outskirts of Rochester, close to his boyhood home of Chatham.

Again, it is possible to see the close relationship between Dickens' life and his work. As mentioned earlier, Pip's home town is based on Rochester. Furthermore, *Great Expectations* centres on Pip's deep and romantic attachment to Estella, thus enabling Dickens to express his own deep and romantic attachment to Ellen Ternan in fictional form. *Our Mutual Friend* (1864–65) also has a deep and romantic attachment at its centre.

In 1870, before he was able to complete his last novel, *Edwin Drood*, Dickens died of a heart attack brought on by overwork. By the time of his death, voting rights had been greatly extended (1867), the practice of imprisonment for debt had been abolished (1869), and Forster's Elementary Education Act (1870) had set about creating the genesis of the state education system that we enjoy today. England still had a deeply unequal and class-ridden society, however, with tremendous excesses of both poverty and wealth, and this would remain unchanged for many decades.

Dickens' world

During Charles Dickens' lifetime, nineteenth-century Britain was under tremendous pressure from the twin forces of science and technology, which generated great social, political and economic changes. These affected the ways in which people viewed both themselves and their relationships with each other, with their religion and with society at large.

Industrialisation

Industrialisation in particular was a destabilising factor that threatened the entire fabric of Victorian England. It created great wealth for a new entrepreneurial minority who were astute enough to set up factories and mills or who created other related businesses that advanced Britain's trade and commerce. Industrialisation, however, also led to a ruthless exploitation of the largely unskilled and uneducated workers, who were needed as manual labour to keep the machines running.

Social unrest

The new factory towns brought large numbers of workers into close proximity. At the same time, workers inevitably became resentful of the poverty and suffering they were forced to endure by the wealthy manufacturers or mill owners who employed them. This had the effect of politicising people. In *Hard Times* (1854), Dickens explicitly explores the plight of people living in English factory towns in coping with the twin evils of poverty and pollution.

The impact of science

Throughout the Victorian era, scientific discoveries began to undermine the traditional Christian beliefs and values that were commonly regarded as essential for social cohesion. The revolutionary thinker Karl Marx had explicitly acknowledged this when he wrote that 'Religion ... is the opium of the people' (1843–44). Marx meant by this that the promise of an afterlife encouraged the poor to suffer the iniquities and inequalities of this life in silence.

Build critical skills

How might the kinds of hardship and injustice undergone by people in developing countries today be compared with those of working-class people in Dickens' time?

One of the biggest challenges to traditional Christianity came with the publication of Charles Darwin's *On the Origin of Species* (1859), in which Darwin argued for a model of the world in which life gradually evolved over an immense period of time. The idea of this incremental process challenged the fundamental Christian belief that God created the Earth and all things in just six days. Darwin's theory, being partly based on fossil evidence, also suggested that the world was many times older than the Bible indicated. If the Bible could not be trusted on the crucial point of the creation of life, what other errors might it contain?

Darwin's findings also suggested a world in which the predominant principle is 'the survival of the fittest'. This is a vision of an uncaring universe in which the weak are destroyed by the strong and in which God does not intervene. A number of these ideas had surfaced prior to Darwin's publication. They had, for instance, obviously influenced the famous poet Alfred Tennyson when he wrote of 'Nature, red in tooth and claw' in his epic poem *In Memoriam* (published in 1850).

The 1851 Census showed that church attendance was in decline. According to the historian H.C.G. Matthew, writing in the *Oxford Illustrated History of Britain*, 'Of potential church-goers, over five and a quarter million stayed at home.' This was out of a combined population of England and Wales of around 18 million. Matthew Arnold lamented this trend towards greater secularisation in his famous poem 'Dover Beach' (1867), when he wrote:

> The Sea of Faith
> Was once, too, at the full, and round earth's shore…
> But now I only hear
> Its melancholy, long withdrawing roar,
> Retreating…

GRADE BOOSTER

A society can be described as secular when it does not place too much importance on religious beliefs and values. Over time, secularisation can lead to a society where atheism or agnosticism is more common than religion. To many Victorians, this prospect was unthinkable. Showing an awareness of this, by referring to how Dickens' heroes and heroines display essentially Christian values, could gain you marks for AO3.

Population growth and urban development

Tremendous population growth during the nineteenth century also placed much pressure on Victorian society. In 1801, according to the official Census of that year, the population of England stood at 8.3 million. By the 1851 Census, it had more than doubled, to 16.92 million. This growth was mainly in the towns and was supplemented by agricultural labourers leaving rural areas in search of higher wages or employment. For the first time in the history of the nation, more people in the UK mainland were living in towns and cities than in the countryside. Great Britain had become the leading manufacturing nation in the world. Again writing in the *Oxford Illustrated History of Britain*, the historian H.C.G. Matthew remarks: 'An urban nation had no precedent: perhaps that was why the British dwelt so tenaciously on rural images and traditions.'

It can be argued that Dickens dwells on rural traditions in *Great Expectations* (1860–61). He deliberately sets his novel at the beginning of the century, when 'Steam, was yet in its infancy' (Chapter 7, p.46). In contrast with some of his other works, this novel does not focus in particular on the malignant physical institutions of Victorian society. Instead, and perhaps more importantly, it considers the condition of the nation's soul, which has allowed such evils to evolve. *Great Expectations* presents a deeply poetic psychological study of a nation gripped by greed and selfishness. This is most powerfully explored through the concept of what it is to be a gentleman.

How relevant is *Great Expectations* today?

Unlike the period when the novel was written, our society provides a welfare state with all the benefits of a state education system, a national health service, social security, old age pensions, universal voting rights and guaranteed human rights. Discrimination on the basis of social class is also less prevalent. This does not mean that there are no problems with debt, injustice or poverty, but the system is in place to prevent these on such a wide scale as in Victorian times.

One similarity with Dickens' time, however, is that our society appears to have replaced an obsession with the social elite of 'high society' with an obsession with the new aristocracy of celebrity. In addition, Pip's search for a meaningful, productive and morally upright life is as important today as it ever has been. The fundamental moral truths that Pip discovers on his way to full maturity help to establish this coming-of-age bildungsroman as the timeless classic that it has become.

The emphasis is on using the background historical information in order to understand the text better and thus to analyse the novel's probable impact on the reader better, although a modern reader of *Great Expectations* will most likely react in a different manner to a

GRADE BOOSTER

A bildungsroman is a novel that explores the development of the personality of the main character. *Great Expectations* can correctly be described as a bildungsroman and, when used relevantly, an examiner will be pleased to see such literary terminology in your work, for example when referring to the key stages in Pip's progress towards moral redemption.

contemporary reader. For example, the class divide between Pip and Estella may not be especially relevant to readers in more democratic societies today, but the timeless theme of unrequited love certainly is.

GRADE *FOCUS*

Grade 5

Grade 5 candidates should 'use understanding of contexts to inform responses to texts'; that is, they should show clear understanding of the social, cultural and historical background of texts and of how these influence their meanings.

Grade 8

Grade 8/9 candidates should 'show perceptive understanding of how contexts shape texts and responses to texts'; that is, they should make perceptive, critical comments about the ways contextual factors influence the choices writers make, and should identify and comment on the impact of the social, cultural and historical background of texts on different readers at different times.

REVIEW YOUR LEARNING

(Answers are given on p. 100.)

1 During which years did Charles Dickens live?

2 In what way is Rochester significant to *Great Expectations*?

3 In what year did the young Charles Dickens and his family move to London?

4 Which two related childhood events are powerfully reflected in a number of Dickens' novels?

5 How might Dickens' personal circumstances have affected the romantic nature of *Great Expectations*?

6 In *Great Expectations*, how might Dickens be responding to his society's increasing lack of religious belief?

Plot and structure

Target your thinking

- When is *Great Expectations* set? (**AO3**)
- How does Dickens distort time within the novel? (**AO2**)
- What are the main events in the novel and when do they occur? (**AO2**)
- How does Dickens create and satisfy suspense? (**AO2**)

Main events

The main events of the novel take place over a period of approximately sixteen years. Dickens' 'Working notes', in which he initially planned out the timescale of the novel, state that 'Pip was about 7 at the opening of the story' (p.510 of the Penguin Classics edition). This is confirmed within the novel itself when Pip tells Herbert in Chapter 50 that he thinks he was in his 'seventh year' when he first encountered Magwitch, although this phrase could equally identify Pip as having been six. At the beginning of Chapter 39, Pip announces that he is 23. This is the year of Magwitch's return, in which he reveals that he is Pip's true benefactor. Most of Volume III relates the events that unfold during the course of this turbulent year.

As Dickens is rather cavalier with his references to time, it is not always possible precisely to locate an event within the internal timeframe of the novel. This is particularly so in Volume I. Pip is indentured to Joe approximately two years after the novel has begun, which would make him nine. According to Dickens' 'Working notes', however, Pip is 'say 18 or 19' (p.509) when he first arrives in London and, as his apprenticeship lasts just short of four years, the age at which he is apprenticed to Joe is more likely to be 14 or 15.

Historical setting

The exact year in which *Great Expectations* begins is also difficult to determine, as it is stated within neither the novel itself nor in Dickens' 'Working notes'. On the opening page of the novel, Dickens simply refers to a time 'long before the days of photographs' (p.3). Other historical information that the mature Pip reveals during the course of his narrative enables the time of the main action to be fixed to the early nineteenth century.

One recurrent form of historical information is the mode of transport that Pip uses when he commutes between London and his home town. He travels to London for the first time at the beginning of Volume II. He states, 'The journey from our town to the metropolis, was a journey of about five hours', and the means of transport was a 'four-horse stage-coach' (Chapter 20, p.163). Railways are never mentioned in the novel and as the first passenger railway opened in 1825, and Britain's rail network was virtually complete by 1850, the reader can clearly see that the young Pip's world is of an earlier period.

Using such historical details as mentioned above, the literary critic Jerome Meckier has concluded that the novel opens on Christmas Eve 1812, which was also the year of Dickens' birth (see the editor's first note to Volume I, Chapter 1, on p.485 of the Penguin Classics edition). Regardless of the exact date, it is clear that *Great Expectations* reflects the time of Dickens' own childhood when he was living in Chatham in Kent during 1817–22, which might be one reason why he has chosen to write the novel from the first-person perspective.

At the time of Dickens' birth the British King, George III, had gone insane and Britain was heavily involved in the Napoleonic Wars, which lasted from 1803–15.

Build critical skills

High-profile television shows such as *12 Monkeys* and *Game of Thrones* create, satisfy and then recreate new strands of suspense as they build towards an end-of-series climax. Chart the progress of one strand of suspense in *Great Expectations*. Do the points of climax always appear at the end of a chapter or volume?

Structure

Great Expectations is divided into three volumes and each volume recounts a discrete phase in Pip's life. The novel was originally published in serial form between December 1860 and August 1861, in weekly instalments in Dickens' own weekly magazine, *All the Year Round*. The serial form required the author to maintain the reader's commitment, hence the continual creation and recreation of suspense. Furthermore, the fact that it was published in December will undoubtedly have influenced Dickens to open the novel on Christmas Eve so as to capitalise on the festive spirit.

Volume I

Chapters 1–6

The novel opens on Christmas Eve with the introduction of the main character, Pip, as a child. The narrative voice is immediately established as a first-person narrator looking back on an early childhood memory.

A sense of foreboding is created by the fact that Pip is visiting a graveyard, which contrasts with the festive nature of the season. The surroundings are made more threatening because 'this bleak place [was] overgrown with nettles...' (Chapter 1, p.3). The fact that his parents are dead establishes Pip as an orphan and so instantly creates sympathy for him. Tension and suspense are introduced when Pip is surprised by a convict, who manhandles him roughly and threatens to cut his throat. Pip's obvious terror heightens the dramatic impact of the situation.

▲ Pip meets Magwitch in the graveyard

The convict, whom we later discover is named Magwitch, terrorises the seven-year-old Pip into agreeing to steal food and a file from his foster parents, Joe and Mrs Joe Gargery. This causes a crisis of conscience in the boy, and creates an internal psychological dynamic that drives the plot throughout most of these early chapters. Pip is torn between his promise to Magwitch and the love and respect he feels for Joe. He is also terrified of being beaten by Mrs Joe should she discover the theft. Mrs Joe's violence is well established in this section and so the reader knows that Pip's fears are well founded. Dickens' treatment of this violence is comical, however, and so is it not as disturbing to the reader as it might otherwise have been.

GRADE BOOSTER

```
You could gain credit by showing an awareness of why
this immediate creation of suspense in Chapter 1 is
essential. The novel appeared in episodes rather like
a modern-day soap opera or long-running drama series
and, therefore, Dickens needed to generate questions
in his readers' minds so that they would follow the
next episode in order to discover the answers.
```

Key quotation

The terrors that had assailed me whenever Mrs. Joe had gone near the pantry, or out of the room, were only to be equalled by the remorse with which my mind dwelt on what my hands had done.

(Chapter 4, p.23)

The suspense aroused by Pip's dilemma is finally resolved in Chapter 5 when Magwitch deliberately takes the blame for the thefts, although Pip's sense of guilt about stealing from Joe persists. The suspense created by the obvious hatred between the two convicts, Magwitch and Compeyson, however, is not resolved. This raises a question in the reader's mind that is not answered until Volume III.

Although the reader is not aware of it yet, Dickens has introduced a plot element that becomes highly significant at the end of Volume I. Pip's 'noble' behaviour has a serious effect on Magwitch, who determines to reciprocate by making Pip a gentleman.

The powerful motif of the 'mist', which symbolises moral blindness, is also introduced in this section. The 'hulks' reinforce this impression and stand as a powerful symbol of crime and punishment.

Hulks: old, disused ships used as floating prisons.

▲ The 'hulks'

Key quotation

The mist was heavier yet when I got out upon the marshes, so that instead of my running at everything, everything seemed to run at me.

(Chapter 3, p.17)

Build critical skills

What do you think the mist symbolises? Why else do you think Dickens uses it here?

GRADE BOOSTER

```
A motif is a recurring image or idea. Try to introduce
literary terminology like this into your responses,
ensuring that you relate it closely to evidence and
your analysis of the text.
```

Chapters 7–13

A year has passed. Dickens now introduces a new situation that generates a new area of suspense for the reader and drives the action in this section of the novel. Pip learns that he is to visit a local rich lady, Miss Havisham, supposedly in order to be a play companion for her adopted young daughter.

Pip arrives at Satis House, a decaying mansion that has a strong Gothic atmosphere to it. He is met by the rude and arrogant Estella, who instantly sets about insulting him. So begins the process of undermining his self-esteem, which ultimately results in his obsession with bettering himself so that he can be worthy of her. Although distressed by her behaviour, Pip is captivated by Estella's beauty and falls instantly in love. This is the start of the romantic interest. The reader's desire to know if Pip will eventually 'win' Estella is one of the most compelling areas of suspense in the novel.

Miss Havisham is immediately established as a fascinating figure who creates significant intrigue by her bizarre appearance and behaviour. Dickens sets about gradually establishing the powerful misconception that she might be intending to advance Pip's prospects in life. This becomes a tremendous source of suspense later on in the novel when Pip does come into his 'great expectations'. Both Pip and the reader are led to believe that his benefactor is Miss Havisham and, therefore, that he must be destined to be with Estella.

Chapter 11 introduces the reader to Herbert Pocket, the 'pale young gentleman' who challenges Pip to fight. Herbert remains an undeveloped character at this stage.

Important themes are introduced in this section, such as revenge and class. As a result of her obsessive desire to avenge herself on all males, Miss Havisham tacitly encourages Estella to make Pip feel ashamed of his working-class roots and so begins his drive to become a gentleman. The run-down condition of both Miss Havisham's appearance and her house, however, send out powerful clues to the reader that Pip's ambition is not worthwhile.

Build critical skills

What are the advantages and disadvantages for a novelist of using a first-person narrator? Should we always assume that the narrator will see things as they really are? How does Dickens successfully mislead the reader about Miss Havisham's intentions for Pip and Estella via his skilful use of a first-person narrator?

GRADE BOOSTER

Dickens uses aspects of the Gothic genre in his portrayal of Miss Havisham and Satis House. It was a style of writing that encompassed such elements as spooky old houses, mad people and mysterious events. Showing (appropriately) in your responses that you understand these Gothic references could establish the quality of your answer.

Key quotation

She seemed much older than I, of course, being a girl, and beautiful and self-possessed; and she was as scornful of me as if she had been one-and-twenty, and a queen.

(Chapter 8, p.56)

Key quotation

Then, he and my sister would pair off in such nonsensical speculations about Miss Havisham, and about what she would do with me and for me...

(Chapter 12, p.97)

Build critical skills

Miss Havisham is an excellent example of Dickens' ability to create suspense not just by plot but also by characterisation. The reader is intrigued to discover why all the clocks have been stopped at 'twenty minutes to nine' and why she is wearing a faded wedding dress. Which other characters will the reader have questions about?

Chapters 14–19

Dickens moves time on again in this section. At the beginning of Chapter 14, approximately one year has passed since Pip's first visit to Satis House. Pip has begun to train as Joe's apprentice but the position that he had long looked forward to is now hateful to him owing to his desire to be worthy of Estella. Estella will not reappear again until Volume II, however, as she has been sent abroad to be educated as a lady. There is a deliberate parallel here in their respective careers that emphasises their different social status.

The important themes of longing to be a gentleman and of self-improvement through education are significantly enhanced in this section. Dickens' writing here is more psychologically- than action-based, as the main dynamic – Pip's struggle to come to terms with his humble life as a blacksmith's apprentice – is in his mind.

Dickens returns to a more robust and action-based plot line at the end of Chapter 15, however, when Mrs Joe has been savagely attacked. In Chapter 16 Biddy declares the culprit to be Orlick but nothing conclusive is given away, again creating an area of suspense that helps to keep the reader engaged.

The plot gathers tremendous pace towards the end of Volume I when Pip is in the fourth year of his apprenticeship. Jaggers suddenly appears in Chapter 18 and announces that Pip has come into 'great expectations' and is to leave for London in a week to become a gentleman. Jaggers' non-committal suggestion of Matthew Pocket, Miss Havisham's relative, as Pip's tutor reopens the romantic suspense of whether Pip will finally obtain Estella. It also reinforces the deliberate deception and encourages the reader to believe that Miss Havisham is Pip's benefactor. As the majority of Dickens' readers were middle class, and as the gap between the classes was huge during the nineteenth century, this would be a moment of great dramatic tension for them.

Pip's attitude and behaviour abruptly become distant to Joe and Biddy as he prepares to move into a much higher level of society, one that would ridicule him for having such humble acquaintances. This is not only the beginning of a new phase in Pip's life but it is also the expansion of one of the novel's major themes and social comments. Through Pip's deplorable attitude towards those who have cared for him, Dickens begins to show the reader the shallow, unproductive and snobbish lifestyle that being a gentleman can involve. It is not until Volume III that Pip comes to a full realisation of this for himself and understands how shameful his ingratitude has been.

Key quotation

I made my exultant way to the old Battery, and, lying down there to consider the question whether Miss Havisham intended me for Estella, fell asleep.

(Chapter 19, p.147)

Key quotation

'Biddy,' I exclaimed, impatiently, 'I am not at all happy as I am. I am disgusted with my calling and with my life. I have never taken to either, since I was bound.'

(Chapter 17, pp.127–28)

Volume II

Chapters 20–26

In Chapter 20, Pip arrives in London and, according to Dickens' 'Working notes', he is 'say 18 or 19' (p.509). Dickens immediately qualifies Pip's excitement at arriving in London by depicting the city as both squalid and frightening. Just as 'mist' is a recurring motif in the marshes of Volume I, 'dirt' is a recurring motif in London. As with the opening to Volume I, death is immediately apparent.

One of Pip's first encounters in London is with the corrupt 'partially drunk minister of justice', who offers to reveal the full brutality of Newgate Prison for a price (Chapter 20, pp.165–66).

Just as there was the dramatic foreshadowing of a gallows looming over Magwitch in Chapter 3 (p.18), so there is a gallows here. By showing the savagery of the judicial system, Dickens is also introducing a theme that becomes extremely important towards the end of Volume III.

The fact that Pip has moved away from the limited confines of his home town allows Dickens to introduce a host of new characters and so generate new areas of interest for the reader. For example, Jaggers' emphatic declaration that he is not permitted to reveal the identity of Pip's benefactor serves to heighten this mystery – and it is not ultimately resolved until the end of this volume.

Chapters 21 and 22 reunite Pip with Herbert Pocket, the two having briefly met at Satis House, when Herbert had challenged Pip to fight. The reader may be surprised to discover that Herbert is not the pugilistic boy of Pip's previous encounter but is now a caring and thoughtful young man. The occasion of their reunion allows Dickens the opportunity to satisfy some of the suspense that has been built up in Volume I and to show that things are not always as they first seemed to Pip. For example, we learn how Miss Havisham was jilted on her wedding day by a heartless opportunist and how she adopted and reared Estella 'to wreak revenge on all the male sex' (Chapter 22, p.177).

Build critical skills

The discrepancy between appearance and reality is a major theme in literature, because the illusion creates additional layers of complexity and interest. Can you think of any other examples of this in the text?

Key quotation

'Well! Joe is a dear good fellow – in fact, I think he is the dearest fellow that ever lived – but he is rather backward in some things. For instance, Biddy, in his learning and his manners.'
(Chapter 19, p.148)

Key quotation

So, I came into Smithfield; and the shameful place, being all asmear with filth and fat and blood and foam, seemed to stick to me.
(Chapter 20, p.165)

Key quotation

As I declined the proposal on the plea of an appointment, he was so good as to take me into a yard and show me where the gallows was kept, and also where people were publicly whipped…
(Chapter 20, p.166)

GRADE BOOSTER

```
Show awareness of your understanding of dramatic
foreshadowing where appropriate to an examination
question. Dickens often provides subtle clues, for
example through imagery which foretells future
events; in Magwitch's case, the gallows are highly
significant. This exemplifies how carefully Dickens
planned his novels.
```

As *Great Expectations* is a first-person narrative, the reader can know only what the narrator knows and so Dickens has to plan for occasional scenes like this in order to relay essential plot information. In the process of answering some questions, however, new ones are created. For instance, what has happened to the man who callously broke Miss Havisham's heart?

Dickens uses this series of chapters in order to introduce such additional characters as Matthew Pocket (Pip's tutor), Startop and Drummle. Drummle is quickly established as an aggressive and mean-spirited individual. He becomes an important plot device in Volume III, when Dickens uses him to drive a seemingly immovable wedge between Pip and Estella. In dramatic terms, this can be termed a 'complication'. A new strand of suspense is also created in Chapter 26 with the introduction of Molly, Jaggers' enigmatic maid.

Build critical skills

Why does Dickens choose to answer some of the questions created in Volume I at this stage of the novel? Could it be to provide the reader with some satisfaction, while simultaneously creating new areas of suspense? Would the reader become bored and dissatisfied if all the answers were delayed to the very end?

This series of chapters is much less dramatic than other sections of the novel and relies quite heavily on comedy for its momentum. Good examples are the hopelessly disorganised Pocket household and the eccentric home of Wemmick, with its incongruous castle-like features and the amiable but deaf 'aged parent'.

Chapters 27–34

Dickens again moves the plot on by reintroducing Estella and Miss Havisham into Pip's life. There is much anticipation as to how Estella will react to Pip now that he is a gentleman and now that she has grown up into a young woman.

Before developing this area of suspense, however, Dickens brings Joe to London to deliver the news of Estella's return from abroad (Chapter 27). This allows Dickens the opportunity to write another memorably comic scene as Joe awkwardly juggles his hat before Pip and Herbert. More importantly, it allows Dickens to highlight Pip's snobbishness and the depth of his ingratitude to Joe. Joe now feels so awkward in Pip's company that he begins the scene by referring to 'Pip' but soon feels compelled to address him as 'Sir', owing to the cold formality of his reception.

The next day Pip hurriedly takes the coach to Satis House but, significantly, rejects Joe again by choosing to stay at the Blue Boar inn. There is a powerful reunion at Satis House in Chapter 29, in which Miss Havisham exhorts Pip to love Estella. Estella, in turn, warns Pip that she is incapable of love. Once again, the romantic interest in the novel becomes suspenseful. Pip clearly hopes that he and Estella are destined to be together, but Estella's declared inability to love creates a tremendous complication that the reader is most eager to have resolved.

Dickens also uses this trip to Satis House to have Pip arrange for Jaggers to sack Orlick from his post as Miss Havisham's gatekeeper. This seemingly minor event will reach a climax towards the end of Volume III, when Orlick tries to murder Pip. Any sense of the future dramatic import of this event is masked, however, by two comic scenes: Trabb's boy ridiculing Pip's social pretentiousness (Chapter 30), and Pip's visit to the theatre in London (Chapter 31) to see Wopsle star in *Hamlet*.

As is often the case with Dickens, the parody of Pip by Trabb's boy has a satirical purpose. As Trabb's boy chants 'Don't know yah!' (Chapter 30, p.246), the reader is reminded of Pip's rejection of Joe and Biddy.

After the comic interlude, which allows Dickens to keep the reader in a state of anticipation, the main plot line involving Estella and Pip is resumed in Chapter 33. Dickens deliberately creates suspense when he has Estella remark: 'We are not free to follow our own devices, you and I' (p.265). By this, Dickens is subtly confirming to the reader Pip's hopeful impression that he and Estella are destined by Miss Havisham to marry. Dickens then almost immediately throws the reader into confusion, however, by re-establishing tension when Estella remarks 'will you never take warning?' (p.268).

Chapters 35–39

Chapter 35 contains the riotously funny description of Mrs Joe's funeral, which includes such comic moments as the bystanders cheering the procession because they are so thrilled by the over-the-top spectacle of the occasion. Dickens, however, also uses the event to remind the reader of Pip's continuing neglect of Joe.

Pip is 'generalising a period of my life' (p.274) in Chapter 34 and, by Chapter 36, two or more years have passed on and Pip is 21. Chapter 36 continues the important theme of Pip's ever-increasing debts. Dickens resumes his social commentary when he has the narrator reveal the ridiculously extravagant and unproductive lifestyle of a gentleman, as Pip and Herbert spiral into debt.

Key quotation

Miss Havisham: 'Love her, love her, love her!'

(Chapter 29, p.239)

Key quotation

Estella: 'You must know… that I have no heart…'

(Chapter 29, p.237)

Key quotation

Pip: 'I love her, I love her, I love her!'

(Chapter 29, p.243)

Build critical skills

A parody is a comical imitation. In what way is Trabb's boy a parody of Pip?

Key quotation

Estella to Pip: "And necessarily," she added, in a haughty tone; "what was fit company for you once, would be quite unfit company for you now."

(Chapter 29, p.237)

Build critical skills

Satire is when a writer uses humour to make a moral point by making fun of the vice or folly of someone or something. What in your opinion is Pip's folly?

The reader is also reminded of Pip's fundamental good nature, however, as in Chapter 37 he uses his wealth to help Herbert to gain an advantageous position in Clarriker's merchant business.

In Chapter 38, Dickens moves time on two years. The tension of the novel's main romantic interest is maintained, as Pip's jealousy intensifies over Estella's increasing circle of male admirers, especially the detestable Drummle. Another source of dramatic interest in this section is the first sign of a rift between Estella and Miss Havisham. This occurs in Chapter 38, when Miss Havisham ironically scolds Estella for her lack of affection.

By Chapter 39, Pip is 23. This chapter does exactly what Chapter 19 did: it ends the volume on a climax related to Pip's great expectations, except this time it dashes rather than exacerbates Pip's hopes. Magwitch's unexpected return on a symbolically stormy night reveals that he, rather than Miss Havisham, is Pip's benefactor. Once again Dickens satisfies an area of suspense for the reader at the end of the volume. But, again, the resolution is really a complication that raises a new question mark over Pip's future with Estella, and this propels the reader into Volume III.

Volume III

Chapters 40–57 deal in great detail with the period from January to June of the year in which Pip has become 23.

Chapters 58–59 cover a period of 11 years and briefly summarise the time leading up to the climactic moment when Pip and Estella unexpectedly meet at the site of the former Satis House and finally become united. Both characters are aged approximately 34.

Chapters 40–44

Despite Magwitch's rough manners, the obvious delight he shows in Pip in Chapter 39 instantly establishes him as a sympathetic figure. Both suspense and concern are generated in Chapter 40 by Pip's discovery of a mysterious figure lurking in the darkness of the staircase only hours after Magwitch's arrival. This creates tension as the reader is aware that Magwitch is an illegal returnee and that he would face the death penalty if caught.

GRADE BOOSTER

```
Examination questions involving the presentation of
character will always ask you to comment on how an
author reveals character, i.e. to respond to AO2.
(For more, see the roation on character on p.31 of
this guide.)
```

Once more Pip is displayed in a poor light, as yet again his ingratitude and snobbery come to the fore. It is important that Dickens establishes Pip's negative reaction to Magwitch at the outset of Volume III. Much of the dramatic interest, as well as the moral message, arising out of the rest of the novel results from the change of attitude that Pip will undergo during the next three months of his life.

Chapter 42 is yet another example of an episode that Dickens deliberately has to create in order to update Pip, and hence the reader, on crucial plot information that has so far been withheld. Magwitch recounts his history with Compeyson, the man we saw him grappling with on the marshes in Chapter 5. We also learn that it was Compeyson who jilted Miss Havisham on her wedding day. This carefully planned revelation allows Dickens to satisfy two significant areas of suspense at one time. The current whereabouts of Compeyson remains a mystery, however, and therefore adds further tension as to the identity of the suspicious lurker in Chapter 40.

Pip's resolution to visit Satis House to say goodbye to Estella creates tremendous anticipation. The reader eagerly looks forward to seeing Pip challenge Miss Havisham over her cruel deception. The confrontation is genuinely electrifying and Miss Havisham displays uncharacteristic signs of guilt. The power of the scene is further enhanced by Estella's revelation that she is to marry Drummle.

Build critical skills

Read the following extract from Chapter 44, page 360: from 'But when I fell into the mistake I have so long remained in…' to 'Waiting until she was quiet again – for this, too, flashed out of her in a wild and sudden way – I went on.' Look carefully at Dickens' use of highly charged emotive vocabulary, for example 'kind', 'snares', 'flashed', 'wild'. Also look at his use of short sentences, longer but heavily punctuated sentences, rhetorical questions and exclamation marks in the dialogue in order to convey both Pip's and Miss Havisham's agitation.

Build critical skills

Read the extract on page 332 of Chapter 40 beginning 'There's something worth spending in that there book…' and ending 'Look over it, dear boy'. Consider the various ways in which Dickens shows Magwitch's self-reproaching humility and obvious affection for Pip, and how this endears Magwitch to the reader.

GRADE BOOSTER

```
You may
well get an
examination
question that
asks you to
demonstrate
your
understanding
of how Dickens
presents Pip's
moral and
psychological
development.
Be prepared
to write
about your
views on this
subject but
make sure you
support them
with textual
evidence.
```

Build critical skills

A rhetorical question is asked to create a desired effect rather than to gain an answer. The expected/preferred answer is assumed. Why do you think writers often use rhetorical questions?

On his return to London at the end of Chapter 44, the suspense regarding Magwitch's safety is immediately reignited as Pip receives a climactic note from Wemmick warning: 'DON'T GO HOME'. As we discover in the next chapter, this is because Wemmick has discovered that Compeyson is pursuing Magwitch.

Chapters 45–49

The focus returns to Magwitch. The reader is reminded of the grave danger that Magwitch is in as Pip and Herbert take enhanced precautions for his safety by removing him to Clara's house. The comic interlude of Wopsle's latest dramatic performance in Chapter 47 is also economically turned back onto the main action as Wopsle informs Pip that during the performance he had recognised a convict (Compeyson) sitting just behind Pip. In Chapter 48, Dickens satisfies a further area of suspense through Pip's certain conviction that Jaggers' maid Molly is Estella's real mother.

GRADE BOOSTER

Throughout *Great Expectations*, comic interludes are often used as a delaying technique in order to keep the reader in suspense as to the next development in the main plot. Look carefully for examples of Dickens using structure in this way.

Chapter 49 returns us to Satis House for another dramatic scene with Miss Havisham. Her remorse for the harm that she has caused to both Pip and Estella is emotionally satisfying for the reader, and the fire creates both a literal and metaphorical climax. It is as if the intense hatred and desire for vengeance that she has harboured throughout the novel has finally consumed her.

Key quotation

In the moment when I was withdrawing my head to go quietly away, I saw a great flaming light spring up. In the same moment, I saw her running at me, shrieking, with a whirl of fire blazing all about her, and soaring at least as many feet above her head as she was high.

(Chapter 49, pp.401–02)

▲ An older Pip on a visit to Miss Havisham

One of the most interesting features of the chapters in this section of the novel is that Pip has become far less egocentric and is now displaying a much deeper concern for others, including Miss Havisham and Magwitch. Pip's compassion for Miss Havisham is particularly admirable considering the way that she has treated him over the course of the novel.

Chapters 50–53

In Chapter 50, Dickens has Herbert relate to Pip more of Magwitch's past. This scene stretches the credibility of the first-person narrator. It involves Pip the narrator many years later recalling in tremendous detail what Herbert is similarly recalling in tremendous detail after his conversation with Magwitch the previous evening. But it is important that both Pip and the reader are given this information at this point because it allows Pip to make the startling deduction that Estella is Magwitch's daughter. Pip has uncovered a secret that had eluded even the astute and resourceful Jaggers.

For the first time, Pip is finally in full possession of the facts regarding Estella and this simultaneously suggests that he has become master of his own destiny, having at long last moved beyond the web of lies and deception that had ensnared him for so long. Pip's caring character is again emphasised in Chapters 51 and 52 when he finalises the financial arrangements that will secure Herbert's future even though his own financial outlook is bleak.

Build critical skills

A literal statement is factually true. A metaphorical statement has a poetic truth rather than a literal truth. Consider how fire is used both literally and metaphorically in Chapter 49 in relation to Miss Havisham.

Having answered most of the outstanding questions raised in the plot, Dickens immediately creates a new source of suspense in the form of the mysterious letter that suggests that if Pip wishes to protect Magwitch then he must return to his home village. Pip responds to the summons forthwith and arrives at the meeting place, the sluice house, after dark later that night. Of course, it is a trap to enable Orlick to wreak a brutal revenge. It is also an opportunity for Dickens to tie up a few other loose ends, such as the identity of Mrs Joe's attacker.

As Orlick prepares to pummel Pip to death, it would appear that there is no escape. Dickens has already laid the ground for his protagonist to be saved, however. He had Pip casually mention at the end of Chapter 52 that he had lost the letter: 'I had previously sought in my pockets for the letter, that I might refer to it again, but I could not find it…' (p.421). This little plot device allows Dickens to stage in Chapter 53 a credible last-minute rescue by Herbert, Startop (a fellow student at Mr Pocket's) and, ironically, Trabb's boy.

Chapters 54–59

Pip's stoicism and his continued concern for Magwitch dominate Chapter 54. Despite his severe burns, Pip perseveres with his intention to board a steamer with Magwitch and leave the country. His good friends Herbert and Startop continue to assist him. Chapter 54 contains a beautiful and sustained description of the River Thames as they row towards what they hope will be safety. Nevertheless, Dickens maintains the tension as Pip the narrator continually reports to the reader the group's fear of being followed.

In order to maximise dramatic intensity, Magwitch is indeed apprehended at the last moment — just as they can see the smoke from the Hamburg steamer. In the violent struggle that follows, Magwitch enacts his revenge upon Compeyson as the latter drowns. This scene closely parallels their fight scene in Chapter 5, but this time Dickens allows the reader the satisfaction of seeing Compeyson receive the fate that he so richly deserves. Compeyson is a particularly interesting character because of the manner in which Dickens primarily reveals his character through the comments of other characters. This scene concludes another strand of the novel with an action-packed climax.

Pip's attachment to Magwitch is made patently clear in Chapters 55 and 56 as he supports Magwitch through his trial and nurses him until his death some ten days later. Chapter 57 reintroduces Joe who, in a parallel scene, nurses Pip and protects him from arrest. By uniting Pip and Joe at this point in the novel, and by highlighting the similarity between them, Dickens shows how far Pip has developed as a moral being since the beginning of Volume III. This is further emphasised by the religious terms that Pip uses to describe Joe.

Protagonist: the principal character in a work of fiction.

Build critical skills

'Irony' has many meanings. Here it means 'the opposite of what might have been expected'. Why is Trabb's boy's involvement in the rescue both ironic and amusing in light of his dislike of Pip?

Stoicism: having the courage and strength of character to endure great suffering, especially admirable when that suffering is on behalf of another person.

Key quotation

Pip about Magwitch: 'For now, my repugnance to him had all melted away, and in the hunted wounded shackled creature who held my hand in his, I only saw a man who had meant to be my benefactor, and who had felt affectionately, gratefully, and generously, towards me with great constancy through a series of years. I only saw in him a much better man than I had been to Joe.'

(Chapter 54, p.446)

Key quotation

After which, Joe withdrew to the window, and stood with his back towards me, wiping his eyes. And as my extreme weakness prevented me from getting up and going to him, I lay there, penitently whispering, 'O God bless him! O God bless this gentle Christian man!'

(Chapter 57, p.463)

The full reconciliation with both Joe and Biddy occurs in Chapter 58 when Pip arrives shortly after their wedding, although there is the slight complication that he had intended to ask Biddy to marry him. The fact that Biddy marries Joe on the day that Pip was going to propose to her is yet another irony. Symbolically, the sun is shining: 'The June weather was delicious' (Chapter 58, p.477). Pip has finally left behind the long winter of disharmony and discontent of his former life and is now able to blossom into the full moral being that Dickens had always intended him to be.

Chapter 59 briefly recounts the next 11 years of Pip's life, in which he goes abroad to work with Herbert and becomes a productive and successful businessman as opposed to the unproductive and debt-ridden gentleman he had once been. The moment of his return to the forge eleven years on is laden with symbolism. It is December, the same month in which Pip's story began some 27 years previously. In one way, the novel has turned full circle as it returns both Pip and the reader to the place and month where it all began. Joe, of course, is sitting by the hearth but this time there is a different Pip and this one is surrounded by the love of Joe and Biddy; there is no Mrs Joe to spoil the picture.

The plot ends on a major coincidence. Pip revisits the site of the former Satis House and there meets Estella, who also has not returned for eleven years. Estella is much wiser and chastened as she too has undergone a long and painful spiritual journey. Their romance is finally resolved at the scene of their first meeting. They are instantly reconciled and the last lines complete the love story that has been the driving force of most of the novel: '...I saw the shadow of no parting from her.'

Key quotation

I went towards them slowly, for my limbs were weak, but with a sense of increasing relief as I drew nearer to them, and a sense of leaving arrogance and untruthfulness further and further behind.

(Chapter 58, p.477)

Build critical skills

Irony again refers to an event being the opposite of what might be expected. Consider how this time, both Pip and the reader are taken by surprise at the news of Biddy's marriage to Joe in Chapter 58.

GRADE *FOCUS*

Grade 5

To achieve Grade 5, students must show a clear and detailed understanding of the whole novel and of the effects created by its structure.

Grade 8

To achieve Grade 8, students' responses will display a comprehensive understanding of explicit and implicit meanings in the novel as a whole and will examine and evaluate the writer's use of structure in detail.

REVIEW YOUR LEARNING

(Answers are given on p. 100.)

1 In what year might the beginning of the novel be set?
2 What age is Pip at the beginning of the novel?
3 Approximately what age is he when he begins his apprenticeship?
4 What does 'suspense' mean?
5 Why does Dickens resolve a number of areas of suspense at fairly early stages in the novel?
6 How do the frequent comic interludes help to create suspense?
7 What genre is Dickens drawing on in his presentation of Miss Havisham and Satis House?
8 What is the main way in which Dickens reveals Compeyson's character?

Characterisation

Target your thinking

- What is the difference between a 'rounded' character and a 'flat' character? (**AO2**)
- Why does Charles Dickens create both types of character? (**AO2**)
- What methods does Dickens use to reveal his characters to the reader? (**AO2**)
- For what purposes does Dickens use his characters? (**AO2**)

Characters and caricatures

In *Great Expectations*, as in all of Charles Dickens' novels, the reader is introduced to a wide array of characters who vary in the degree to which they can be acknowledged as fully developed individuals. Dickens' 'rounded' characters are the fuller, three-dimensional figures, such as Pip and Estella. They resemble real people in that they are composed of many different personality traits which often conflict. Importantly, rounded characters are capable of change and growth. These tend to be the characters with whom we, as readers, are most emotionally involved.

There is another, far more populous, species of character in *Great Expectations*, however: the caricatures. A few of these are more developed and rounded than the others, a good example being Joe. Generally, however, the caricatures are creatures who do not show much, if any, insight into the true nature of others or themselves. Therefore, their comments on the purpose of life, or on the merits and demerits of other characters within the novel, can rarely be trusted.

The caricatures are 'stock' characters who are rarely capable of change. The caricatures exhibit a restricted range of human thought, emotion and behaviour and are essentially used to illustrate a limited number of human characteristics, such as greed, envy and self-interest. They are frequently employed in order to highlight a moral point or theme that the author wishes to express to the reader and they are often satirised and ridiculed for their own moral short-sightedness.

Such caricatures include Mrs Joe and Pumblechook. As well as providing moral instruction, both of these characters also help to create humour.

GRADE **BOOSTER**

When writing about character, it is important to show
the examiner that you understand that characters
are not real people but are instead creations of
the author, which have been designed partly for the
purposes of advancing the plot or developing themes.

There are also the 'darker' caricatures, such as Compeyson and Orlick.
Both of these characters demonstrate that sin results in either death or
imprisonment and their impact on the reader is designed to be much
more serious. They help to create suspense because of the threat that
they pose to the more sympathetic personalities within the novel.
Furthermore, they fill the reader with a sense of moral outrage because of
their cruel mistreatment of others.

GRADE **BOOSTER**

Try to demonstrate an awareness that stock characters
are a form of caricature. Orlick and Compeyson, for
example, are stock villains, whereas Wopsle is a
stock fool.

How Dickens reveals character

The personality of a character can be revealed in a variety of ways:

- Through their actions – what the character does and how this affects
  other characters, for good or ill.
- Through their dialogue – what the character says and what other
  characters say about that character.
- Through their thoughts – the secret unexpressed hopes, desires and
  perceptions that the character may inwardly conceive but does not
  wish to divulge to other characters. Of course, these are more
  difficult to reveal in a first-person narrative like *Great Expectations* as
  the narrator can really have a detailed knowledge only of his or her
  own thoughts and feelings. The reader is unlikely to tolerate too high
  a level of intuitive guesswork regarding the thoughts and feelings
  of other characters. Such a god-like omniscience (all-encompassing
  knowledge) is more the preserve of a third-person narrator.
- Through the narrator – the observations of the narrator on the
  personality and behaviour of other characters.
- Through the author's use of imagery (metaphors, similes and
  personifications).

Great Expectations is a first-person narrative and, therefore, the reader should be wary of taking all of Pip's comments at face value. Dickens, however, is clearly presenting the Pip who relates the story as an individual who has arrived at a deep spiritual and moral awareness and who is, therefore, somebody the reader can trust, even though in his younger years he makes some understandable mistakes.

The character analyses that follow present evidence derived from all of the above ways in which Dickens reveals his major characters to the reader.

Pip

- Makes tremendous moral and spiritual growth throughout the novel.
- Has a natural nobility of speech and manner despite his humble origins.
- Has a strong sense of right and wrong and is very much affected by conscience.
- Falls deeply in love with Estella at first sight.
- Desperately wishes to become a gentleman so as to be worthy of Estella's higher social status.
- Suffers much unhappiness and dissatisfaction as a result of his infatuation with Estella.
- Becomes corrupted by the shallow values of status and wealth as he aspires to rise in society.
- Ultimately becomes ashamed of his own ungrateful and ungenerous behaviour towards Joe and Biddy.
- Rediscovers the naturally affectionate nature of his original childhood self.

Pip's name may well be symbolic of the emotional, intellectual and spiritual growth that he makes throughout the novel, a pip being a seed. This ability to evolve and grow distinguishes him from most of the other characters, who largely remain static.

Build critical skills

The technique of giving a character a name that reflects their personality or appearance is known as charactonym. Try to find other examples of this technique in the novel.

> **GRADE BOOSTER**
>
> Dickens often associates his characters with images that provide a strong clue as to their respective personalities, for example Pip's own name. Showing an understanding of this in your exam responses will improve your mark for AO2.

Symbol: the use of something concrete, for example the name 'Pip', to represent something abstract, for example spiritual growth. It is a way of representing an idea more vividly (clearly) and more poetically.

In the opening sentence, Pip immediately introduces himself as the novel's narrator and sets about recounting the chance encounter with Magwitch that ultimately determines his fate. The older narrator describes his younger self as 'the small bundle of shivers' (Chapter 1, p.4) who studies the graves of both of his parents and all five of his brothers. A number of sympathetic circumstances are immediately established: he is an orphan, he is frightened by the stormy weather, and he is about to be roughly manhandled by an apparently fierce and murderous convict.

In his dealings with the convict Magwitch, Pip's essentially virtuous nature is instantly established. In response to Magwitch's rough questioning, the young Pip truthfully and respectfully recounts his family circumstances, while simultaneously revealing a degree of spirit and courage that gains the reader's respect:

> I was dreadfully frightened, and so giddy that I clung to him with both hands, and said, 'If you would kindly please to let me keep upright, sir, perhaps I shouldn't be sick, and perhaps I could attend more.'
>
> (Chapter 1, p.5)

GRADE BOOSTER

Notice Dickens' skilful use of dialogue to immediately establish character. It is one of the techniques you should refer to and exemplify in the exam if asked to comment on how Dickens reveals character.

The young Pip's words reveal impeccable good manners, a mature vocabulary and a sophisticated use of grammar that is generally lacking in Dickens' lower-class characters. This contrasts sharply with the clumsy sentence structures and often inaccurately pronounced vocabulary that Magwitch uses to terrorise Pip.

Through his absolute terror of Magwitch, Pip is forced to enter into a pact involving the theft of food and a file from his foster parents, Joe and Mrs Joe Gargery. This promise causes an internal moral conflict that results in such an extreme degree of distress that it drives the plot for the first five chapters. Because the young Pip has such a highly developed sense of right and wrong, he is torn between keeping his promise to Magwitch and stealing from his beloved Joe. Dickens depicts this moral dilemma with an intensity far beyond what would be expected of a child of just seven years of age. Pip the narrator describes how his younger self agonises over 'the dreadful pledge I was under to commit a larceny on those sheltering premises...' (Chapter 2, p.10).

The next significant event in Pip's moral and spiritual evolution is his first encounter with Estella at Satis House. This meeting proves to be the cause of young Pip's dissatisfaction with his life. Almost immediately, he begins to lose sight of his own moral compass and of the moral superiority of the person who had hitherto been most important to him, his loving but child-like foster father, Joe.

His first encounter with Estella and Miss Havisham deludes him into mistaking arrogance and cruelty for superiority. This, combined with the young Estella's great beauty, results in an infatuation that prevails throughout the rest of the novel and which, until the latter stages, becomes the guiding principle that motivates Pip to seek social status over truth and integrity. Consequently, his proposed future as an apprentice at the forge, which had long been the dream of both Pip and Joe, now becomes viewed as demeaning.

As Pip's sense of shame at the sturdiness of Joe's working boots and the roughness of his skilled blacksmith's hands suggests, only the shallow and unproductive life of a gentleman will suffice. Of course, Pip the narrator recognises the lack of wisdom in his younger self's hotly declared adolescent ambition, when he immediately qualifies it as being a 'lunatic confession...' (Chapter 17, p.129).

Towards the end of Volume I, Pip's wish to be a gentleman is indeed granted, this being part of the fairy-tale quality of the novel. As in most fairy tales, however, it is wise to be careful what you wish for. The life of a gentleman, as depicted in Volume II, leads Pip into irresponsibly extravagant ways, which quickly result in debt, depression and a lack of direction and satisfaction. Worse still, Pip's extravagant lifestyle also leads to the corruption of his best friend, the otherwise virtuous Herbert Pocket. Through Pip's severe lapses in both judgement and behaviour, Dickens demonstrates the moral inadequacies of the upper-class society into which Pip has successfully moved.

Ultimately, what restores Pip to the upright moral certainties that he possessed as a child is the knowledge that his status as a gentleman is founded on the wealth of an ex-convict. As a result, his social standing is invalid in the eyes of the snobbish upper-class world to which he has aspired. Furthermore, Pip now realises that his wealth does not derive from Miss Havisham, as he had mistakenly believed. Pip the narrator explains how it became apparent to his younger self that his hopes had all been 'a mere dream; Estella not designed for me...' (Chapter 39, p.323). The immediate realisation that follows, now that the illusion has been dispelled, is that of his own 'worthless conduct' towards Joe and Biddy (Chapter 39, p.323).

The return of this instinctive sense of right and wrong, which Pip had possessed as a child, becomes the guiding principle that steers him through Volume III, the concluding part of the novel. Pip shows compassion and affection towards the ex-convict Magwitch, secretly ensures that Herbert's fortunes are advanced, generously forgives Miss Havisham for the misery she has caused him, and reconciles himself with both Joe and Biddy, whom he now views with the respect that their upright characters so clearly deserve.

His reward for the painful spiritual journey that he has undertaken during the course of the novel is his ultimate union with his heart's desire – Estella – but not with the unfeeling damaged child of Satis House. He is to be accompanied through the rest of his life by a mature woman who, through her own painful progress, has now learnt the innate value of the unconditional love that Pip has long offered. As she openly declares

GRADE BOOSTER

When writing about character in the exam, you are more likely to gain a higher grade if you use terms that show a precise understanding of specific aspects of personality: for example, for Pip words such as 'innocent' and 'naïve' instead of 'good'.

Key quotation

'And Joe and Biddy both, as you have been to church to-day, and are in charity and love with all mankind, receive my humble thanks for all you have done for me, and all I have so ill repaid!' (Chapter 58, p.479)

GRADE BOOSTER

The examiner will be impressed by an analysis of Pip that looks beyond his personality in order to consider how Dickens uses this character for ulterior purposes such as developing theme, for example the theme of how shallow and pointless the upper class can be.

herself, it is a love that she had once 'thrown away when … quite ignorant of its worth' (Chapter 59, p.484). The journey that Pip has shared with the reader illustrates the novel's essential moral theme: that it is the quality of the individual that really counts, not the eminence of their social position.

Estella

- Adopted and educated by Miss Havisham to break men's hearts.
- Beautiful.
- Proud and arrogant.
- Indifferent to her own fate and that of others.
- Under the direction of Miss Havisham for most of the novel.
- Eventually breaks free from Miss Havisham's control but only to make a disastrous marriage to Bentley Drummle.
- Exhibits emotional and spiritual growth as a result of her own pain and suffering.
- Ultimately comes to recognise the value of such powerful and positive emotions as love, forgiveness and remorse.

Estella is the heroine of *Great Expectations*. She is one of the few characters who is never mocked by Dickens' ironic narrative voice. As a result, there is a genuine element of tragedy about Estella, which arises from her status as the victim of Miss Havisham's obsessive and pathological desire for vengeance. Estella, the natural daughter of Magwitch and Molly, was adopted by Miss Havisham at the age of three in order to become a weapon against men. As Herbert says:

> 'That girl's hard and haughty and capricious to the last degree, and has been brought up by Miss Havisham to wreak revenge on all the male sex.'
>
> (Chapter 22, p.177)

By this point in the novel, Herbert's assessment of Estella's character has been well confirmed to the reader by her previous behaviour towards Pip. When the two meet as children she treats him with condescension, contempt and cruelty. At their first encounter, she insolently demands to know 'Why don't you cry?' (Chapter 8, p.65). At their second meeting, the mature Pip narrates that 'she slapped my face with such force as she had' (Chapter 11, p.82), as Dickens establishes that she is consistently insulting.

She then disappears from Pip's life for an unspecified period of years. While Pip has become Joe's apprentice, Miss Havisham triumphantly declares that Estella has been sent abroad:

> 'Abroad … educating for a lady; far out of reach; prettier than ever; admired by all who see her.'
>
> (Chapter 15, p.116)

Key quotation

Pip explains to Biddy: 'The beautiful young lady at Miss Havisham's, and she's more beautiful than anybody ever was, and I admire her dreadfully, and I want to be a gentleman on her account.'

(Chapter 17, p.129)

▲ Estella and Pip

Miss Havisham's cruel assertion that Estella is far beyond Pip's grasp may also provide the reader with a clue to the charactonym of her name: 'Estella' means star-like. This deliberate symbolism is reinforced during Pip's first visit to Satis House when Pip the narrator describes how 'her light came along the long dark passage like a star' (Chapter 8, p.59). The image is continued when Pip describes how it was 'as if she were going out into the sky' (Chapter 8, p.64).

On her return from France as a young lady of approximately 20, there appears to be a marked improvement in Estella's demeanour. Her manners and behaviour are now those of an apparently sophisticated young lady rather than of a spiteful and spoilt child. On meeting her again at Satis House, Pip the narrator comments on how Estella was 'condescending to me as a brilliant and beautiful woman might' (Chapter 29, p.237). Beneath the veneer, however, is the damaged child who still is incapable of adult empathy, understanding and attachment.

Key quotation

...suffering has been stronger than all other teaching, and has taught me to understand what your heart used to be. I have been bent and broken, but – I hope – into a better shape.

(Chapter 59, p.484)

By the end of the novel, however, Estella has grown into a mature woman as a result of the brutal nature of her marriage to Drummle. Consequently, she is capable of recognising the value of Pip's love and

Key quotation

...I thought long after I laid me down, how common Estella would consider Joe, a mere blacksmith: how thick his boots, and how coarse his hands.

(Chapter 9, p.72)

Key quotation

'Oh! I have a heart to be stabbed in or shot in, I have no doubt,' said Estella, 'and, of course, if it ceased to beat I should cease to be. But you know what I mean. I have no softness there, no – sympathy – sentiment – nonsense.'

(Chapter 29, p.237)

The most appropriate definition for the way **irony** has been used here would be 'contradiction'.

Key quotation

...she had the appearance of having dropped, body and soul, within and without, under the weight of a crushing blow.

(Chapter 8, p.61)

so finally is worthy to be his companion. Her painful journey, however, illustrates the heart-felt Dickensian theme of how adults often damage children as they mindlessly pursue their own agendas.

Miss Havisham

- Wealthy heiress and inheritor of a brewery business that she has allowed to fall into disuse.
- Locked in a time warp stemming from the exact moment at which she was jilted at the altar by Compeyson on her birthday.
- Reclusive and lives in a virtual prison of her own making.
- Fundamentally motivated by her desire 'to wreak revenge on all the male sex'.
- Egocentric and incapable of empathy until near the end of her life.
- Mentally ill and most likely anorexic.

Miss Havisham's name may be symbolic, being a compound of the verb 'have' and the noun 'sham', meaning something false. The irony of 'having' fits in well with the name of her mansion, Satis House – *satis* being Latin for 'enough'. Materially, Miss Havisham can have anything she wants, but spiritually she is clearly impoverished. Through his characterisation, Dickens demonstrates to the reader an essential moral message/theme – that wealth is not enough and that, without love, money is not worth having.

Blinded by hate, Miss Havisham wilfully chooses to live in the moment of the greatest crisis of her life, that being twenty minutes to nine on an unspecified birthday sometime in the past, when Compeyson cruelly jilted her. This is signalled by a number of facts: all of her clocks have been stopped at this time, she still wears her now heavily decaying wedding dress, and the wedding table remains set with a rotting wedding cake at its centre.

Her physical appearance is denoted at various times in the novel by such words as 'skeleton' (Chapter 8, p.58), 'corpse-like' (Chapter 8, p.60), 'grave-clothes' (Chapter 8, p.60) and 'spectre' (Chapter 17, p.125). The impression is of an under-nourished recluse whose only release from her insanity will be death. Her emaciation may well be a result of an eating disorder, to which Jaggers refers when, as Pip the narrator recalls, 'he asked me how often I had seen Miss Havisham eat and drink...' (Chapter 29, p.241).

Build critical skills

How else does Dickens use food to reveal character? Look, for example, at the theft of the pork pie and other items for Magwitch in Chapters 2 and 3, and the Christmas feast in Chapter 4.

Dickens subtly develops the connection between Miss Havisham, food and death in a variety of ways. On the table where the uneaten wedding cake decays (uneaten, that is, apart from the gnawing of hungry mice), Miss Havisham expects to be laid out when dead (Chapter 11, p.89). On the previous page (Chapter 11, p.88), she envisages how her grasping relatives will 'come to feast upon me' once she is dead. And much later in the novel, Dickens extends the metaphor when he has Pip the narrator describe Miss Havisham's desperate admiration of Estella as being as if 'she were devouring the beautiful creature she had reared' (Chapter 38, p.302).

> **Metaphor:** a comparison in which one thing is said to be another thing which it literally is not, or when a thing is described as doing something which it is normally not literally possible to do. In this instance, Miss Havisham's relatives will not literally 'feast' upon her corpse.

GRADE *BOOSTER*

```
There are various reasons why a writer might use a
metaphor but, in general, they are used to create a
more vivid picture of the original thing that is being
described to the reader. Metaphors can also make the
writing more poetic, humorous or dramatic.
```

This pattern of cannibalistic imagery powerfully associates Miss Havisham's psychological and spiritual starvation with Compeyson's cynical rejection of her on her wedding day. It also links this rejection with her equally cynical exploitation of Estella. Furthermore, it helps to portray Miss Havisham as another genuinely tragic figure who, like Estella, is spared the comic mocking narrative tone to which so many of the other characters are subjected.

Dickens underlines both the physical and spiritual deterioration of Miss Havisham in his characterisation of Satis House. The once-thriving brewery has now fallen into disuse and both the grounds and the buildings are heavily neglected. Pip the narrator portrays it as a 'dismal' property, which is 'rustily barred' (Chapter 8, p.55) and has a 'rank garden' full of 'tangled weeds' (Chapter 8, p.64).

Again, the imagery used here is intentional. The frequent references to 'wilderness' and 'weeds' are emblematic of humanity's great 'fall'. There is a biblical echo here of Adam and Eve, who were corrupted by Satan and so fell from grace, ultimately being expelled from the Garden of Eden to the wilderness beyond. The wilderness imagery thus points to the moral corruption of Miss Havisham. The frequent references to bars suggest the way in which Miss Havisham has made herself a prisoner of the painful rejection that she cannot overcome.

▲ Miss Havisham

Build critical skills

Read the description of Miss Havisham on page 60 (Chapter 8), from 'It was then I began to understand...' to '...would have struck her to dust'. Compare this with the description of the wedding dining room in Satis House on page 84 (Chapter 11): 'I crossed the staircase landing...' to '...transpired in the spider community'. Consider how many parallels Dickens has intentionally created between Miss Havisham and her house in these two extracts.

It is only when she is close to death and, as she prophesied, is laid out on her bridal table, that she finally is able to comprehend the extent of the harm that she has inflicted on both Pip and Estella. Her last words to Pip are an impassioned plea for forgiveness (Chapter 49, p.403).

Joe Gargery

- Comically clumsy and awkward, in both manner and speech.
- Has a natural nobility.
- Unconditionally loving and nurturing.
- Subservient to Mrs Joe.
- A formidable opponent to anybody else when roused.

Joe is one of the many static characters who do not alter, apart from by ageing, during the course of the novel. His main function is to highlight Pip's moral deterioration after he becomes a gentleman and rejects Joe for being a social embarrassment. Also, as with Magwitch, Joe is further evidence of the important social theme: that goodness is not tied to class.

Dickens' characterisation of Joe is complicated, however, by the fact that the narrative voice of the mature Pip veers between gross comic ridicule and sincere and reverential respect, a good example of the latter being in Chapter 18 when Pip the narrator refers to Joe's tender touch as being like 'the rustle of an angel's wing!' (Chapter 18, p.141).

Joe is a blacksmith and is married to Pip's elder sister, who savagely dominates the two of them through a combination of random violence and verbal humiliation. She treats both the seven-year-old Pip and the adult Joe as children and Joe readily responds to that status, blithely repeating the mantra 'ever the best of friends'.

Build critical skills

Consider how Dickens frequently presents Joe as a model of Christian virtue for Victorian readers of the novel. Find examples of Christian imagery in the characterisation of Joe to support this reading of him.

True to his subordinate status within his own house, he is completely unable to protect either himself or Pip from Mrs Joe's habitual use of Tickler. This potential moral lapse on the part of the otherwise saintly Joe is justified in Chapter 7 (pp.49–50), when Joe explains how the memory of his abusive father towards his mother inhibits him from taking a stand, lest he too should become an abusive husband.

The paradox, however, is that despite this cowering subservience to Mrs Joe, Joe is the only character in the novel to intimidate the formidable Jaggers (Chapter 18, p.142). He is also able physically to subdue the powerful and brutal Orlick (Chapter 15, p.115).

As a result of his great timidity and frequent verbal and physical clumsiness, Joe readily becomes the object of the narrator's satirical wit. His greatly exaggerated mispronunciations of such words as 'outdacious' (Chapter 9, p.72) and 'architectooralooral' (Chapter 27, p.222) are regularly used for comic effect. He also has a habit of repeating words or phrases obsessively, for example the word 'bolt' in Chapter 2, which gives him an imbecilic air. His sentences are often also long and rambling as he awkwardly struggles to come to the point.

When Dickens chooses to do so, however, the same character can be remarkably wise and astute, as in Chapter 15 (p.110) when he advises the adolescent Pip of the impropriety of visiting Miss Havisham again as she may suspect his motives. He is also quick to realise that the change in Pip's social status after he moves to London makes their association both uncomfortable and undesirable (Chapter 27, p.224).

As well as a natural wisdom, Joe has an innate nobility lacking in so many of the novel's characters, which, for example, makes him appreciate the value of love over money, hence his rejection of Jaggers' offer of twenty guineas in return for Pip's freedom from his apprenticeship (Chapter 18, p.141).

The depth of unconditional love that Joe offers to Pip is symbolised by fire, not just the fire in the forge where Joe pursues his trade but also the fire in the hearth, at which he and the young Pip used to sit. Joe is the young Pip's only source of warmth and affection in a world that is both literally and metaphorically cold. It is no accident, therefore, that when the mature Pip returns to the forge after eleven years of living abroad, he finds Joe once again by his hearth but, this time, in the company of Pip junior.

Abel Magwitch

- Pip's mysterious benefactor.
- Victim both of society and of Compeyson.
- Common-law husband of Molly, Jaggers' maid.
- Transported for life to Australia.
- Becomes a wealthy sheep farmer and stock breeder.
- Estella's real father, though this is not revealed until late in the novel.

Magwitch's first name, Abel, is another example of Dickens' use of charactonym. Although Magwitch may look like a desperate murderer at various points in the novel, his forename identifies him as a victim as opposed to a slayer. Cain and Abel were sons of Adam and Eve, and it was Cain who committed the first ever murder when he killed his brother. The biblical Abel is also a shepherd, which further strengthens the comparison. The religious symbolism inherent in this name ties in well with Dickens' deliberate use of the marshes, which suggest the hostile world to which Adam and Eve (and all mankind) were expelled after their rebellion against God. This is the morally flawed, fallen world that humanity has inherited. Hence the references in Chapter 5 to a 'dismal wilderness' with its 'wicked Noah's ark'.

Key quotation

'If you can't get to be oncommon through going straight, you'll never get to do it through going crooked.'
(Chapter 9, p.72)

GRADE BOOSTER

Imagery refers to the use of such techniques as metaphor and simile. An imagery pattern is when an image is repeatedly used within a text in order to reinforce an impression of someone or something. Examiners are impressed if you are able to write about stylistic features.

Magwitch is another of the limited number of characters in *Great Expectations* who grow through time. He is crucial to the development of the plot as he is the unnamed benefactor behind Pip's sudden change in circumstances. Furthermore, because he insists on secrecy, Magwitch's structural role in the novel is to enable both Pip and the reader to be misled into assuming that Miss Havisham is the benefactor and, more importantly, into assuming that it is Miss Havisham who has ultimately destined Pip to be betrothed to Estella. As well as helping to drive the action of the entire novel, Magwitch also provides much of the tension and suspense that engage the reader's interest in the opening chapters.

On his first appearance, Magwitch is a desperate figure, prepared to cut the throat of a young child (Chapter 1, p.4). Dickens subtly maintains sympathy for him, however, by referring to his hunger, his various wounds and his uncontrollable shivering. His second meeting with Pip (Chapter 3, p.19) reveals a gentle and more gracious nature as he politely thanks Pip for the food. His violent struggle with Compeyson (Chapter 5, p.36), however, reminds us that this is a dangerous man.

Magwitch is soon transported to Australia for the various crimes he committed with Compeyson and, once there, he makes a fortune. He risks all some 16 years later, to return to England to reveal himself as Pip's true benefactor. The reader's first impression of him at this point is not favourable. Dickens purposefully reminds us of his violent past by the fact that he frequently brandishes a knife and utters such threatening statements as 'don't catch hold of me. You'd be sorry arterwards...' (Chapter 39, p.315). The most disturbing aspect of his character, however, is his controlling sense of proprietorship over Pip: 'If I ain't a gentleman ... I'm the owner of such' (Chapter 39, p.321). It is also clear that his motives for advancing Pip are essentially self-serving and are bound up in his desire to assert his supremacy over an established order that has previously made him feel powerless and inferior.

It is not long, though, before Dickens tones down these initial blusters of arrogance and bravado to reveal a man who has greatly mellowed as a result of the hardships of his life. As Herbert remarks to Pip, 'I thought he was softened when I last saw him' (Chapter 50, p.405).

His reasons for making Pip a gentleman are also revised in a way that creates compassion for Magwitch. It becomes clear that he was moved by the young Pip's loyalty towards him and that Pip's sincerity rekindled the love that he felt for his own lost daughter, whom he believes to be dead until the very last moments of his life when Pip reveals that she is a beautiful and wealthy lady.

Magwitch gains most sympathy at the end of the novel, when he is once again betrayed by the villain Compeyson just as he is on the point of escaping to safety. The severe injuries that he sustains while avenging

Key quotation

'...blast you every one, from the judge in his wig, to the colonist a stirring up the dust, I'll show a better gentleman than the whole kit on you put together!'

(Chapter 40, p.332)

Build critical skills

Read Magwitch's account of his early life on pages 346–47 (Chapter 42), beginning 'Dear boy and Pip's comrade...' and ending '...wore out my good share of key-metal still'. Consider the various ways in which society has failed Magwitch and thus driven him to crime.

himself on Compeyson, and his harsh treatment by a judicial system that would prefer to hang him before he can die of his life-threatening injuries, ensure his full rehabilitation in the eyes of the reader. Magwitch represents the theme of the essential goodness of a common man despite all of the social disadvantages that he has faced in life. Dickens has clearly designed him as a deliberate contrast to the corrupt and immoral behaviour of such social 'superiors' as Compeyson and Miss Havisham.

Magwitch is also crucial in Pip's rehabilitation. Pip's compassion and recognition of Magwitch's worth as a human being finally put an end to the superficial snobbery that has beset him since he became a gentleman. By the end, not only is Pip able to appreciate Magwitch's humanity, he has also learnt to appreciate the moral superiority of Joe and Biddy and, hence, the shame of his own ingratitude towards them.

Key quotation

...he pondered over the question whether he might have been a better man under better circumstances. But, he never justified himself by a hint tending that way, or tried to bend the past out of its eternal shape.
(Chapter 56, p.456)

GRADE *FOCUS*

Grade 5

To achieve Grade 5, students will demonstrate a clear understanding of how and why Dickens uses language, form and structure to create characters, supported by appropriate references to the novel.

Grade 8

To achieve Grade 8, students will examine and evaluate the ways that Dickens uses language, form and structure to create characters, supported by thoughtfully chosen and well-integrated references from the novel.

REVIEW YOUR LEARNING

(Answers are given on p.100.)

1 Name three of the methods that Charles Dickens uses to reveal his characters.

2 What does 'charactonym' mean?

3 Which of the characters reviewed in this section develop or change?

4 What changes take place in Pip during the course of the novel?

5 In what ways could Miss Havisham and Estella be seen as the victims of others?

6 What themes or ideas might Magwitch represent?

Themes

Target your thinking

- What are the main themes in *Great Expectations*? (**AO2**)
- How do these themes relate to each other? (**AO2**)
- How do these themes relate to the characters? (**AO2**)

A theme in a novel is an idea that the author explores through such means as character, plot and language. In Dickens' case, the themes that he examines are usually in order to advise the reader on a moral point and, consequently, there is bound to be some overlap between them. Here is a list of some important themes in *Great Expectations*:

- Gentility and social class
- Education
- Justice and mercy
- Romantic love
- Forgiveness and redemption

Gentility and social class

One of the most important themes in *Great Expectations* is that of social status and, in particular, what it means to be a gentleman – or a lady. The lust for greater status is established in the second chapter with the entrance of Mrs Joe, who caustically comments, 'It's bad enough to be a blacksmith's wife (and him a Gargery) without being your mother' (Chapter 2, p.9). This is a preoccupation for Mrs Joe and recurs again in Chapter 4 when she laments, 'Perhaps if I warn't a blacksmith's wife...' (p.22). In fact, it is through her similarly snobbish and aspiring Uncle Pumblechook that the connection with Miss Havisham is first made. As these are two equally unpleasant characters, it is immediately clear that Dickens is condemning such social aspirations. Mrs Joe and Pumblechook are essentially self-seeking and self-serving individuals and, therefore, any rise in their status would not be used for the general good.

GRADE BOOSTER

Although the exam boards tend to set questions on either themes or characters, it is important to realise that this division is quite artificial. Characters are one method by which an author develops themes.

Pip's introduction to the supposedly genteel world of Satis House is a most unpleasant experience. Gentility is demonstrated to be little more than an excuse to belittle those with lesser fortunes and status. It is explicitly associated with materialism, snobbery, vanity, cruelty, superficiality and injustice. This is evidently a lesson that Miss Havisham has taught Estella. With Miss Havisham's approval, Estella instantly sets about humiliating Pip, calling him 'a common labouring-boy' and complaining that 'He calls the knaves, Jacks' (Chapter 8, p.60), thus illustrating the subtle ways in which a person's use of language can define their social class. Pip is then reminded of his place in society when Miss Havisham instructs Estella to 'Let him have something to eat' (Chapter 8, p.62), exactly as though he were a servant. The result of this experience is Pip's distress and the start of his unsettling feelings of inadequacy and dissatisfaction with his position in life.

Key quotation

I took the opportunity of being alone in the court-yard, to look at my coarse hands and my common boots. My opinion of those accessories was not favourable. They had never troubled me before, but they troubled me now, as vulgar appendages. I determined to ask Joe why he had ever taught me to call those picture-cards, Jacks, which ought to be called knaves. I wished Joe had been rather more genteelly brought up, and then I should have been so too.

(Chapter 8, p.62)

It is, of course, such superficial qualities of gentility as appearance and vocabulary that have been impressed upon him rather than anything solid or worthwhile. When Pip describes Estella to Biddy, Dickens is able to offer a more mature and considered viewpoint. Biddy's opinion is that if Pip's aspiration to be a gentleman is because he wishes to 'gain' Estella, then 'she was not worth gaining over' (Chapter 17, p.129). The narrator confirms the validity of Biddy's conclusion by stating 'Biddy was the wisest of girls...' (Chapter 17, p.129). Biddy offers further insights on the topic of gentility when she remarks 'a gentleman should not be unjust neither...' (Chapter 19, p.150).

Herbert and Matthew Pocket are two more characters whose opinions the reader is encouraged to value, and they also offer insights into what being a gentleman should mean.

The reason why Pip aspires to a higher social stratum is in order to obtain the morally inferior but captivatingly beautiful Estella. Once Pip finally attains the status that he so desires, Estella remains beyond his reach and the world of a gentleman is shown to be a shallow and pointless existence that leads only to debt and moral degradation. (For a fuller analysis of this point, see the character analysis of Pip on page 33 of this guide.)

Key quotation

Herbert, quoting his father, tells Pip: '...no man who was not a true gentleman at heart, ever was, since the world began, a true gentleman in manner.'

(Chapter 22, p.181)

Simile: a comparison in which one thing is said to be 'like' or 'as' another thing. Writers use similes (and metaphors) in order to create a clearer and more vivid (visual) impression of the original thing that they are trying to describe to the reader.

Key quotation

I had heard of her as leading a most unhappy life, and as being separated from her husband, who had used her with great cruelty, and who had become quite renowned as a compound of pride, avarice, brutality, and meanness.

(Chapter 59, p.482)

Key quotation

He set up fur a gentleman, this Compeyson, and he'd been to a public boarding-school and had learning. He was a smooth one to talk, and was a dab at the ways of gentlefolks.

(Chapter 42, p.347)

As Dickens demonstrates through his characterisation of tradespeople such as Trabb, however, society values money and status rather than innate nobility: 'So, Mr. Trabb measured and calculated me, in the parlour, as if I were an estate…' (Chapter 19, p.152). This simile makes Trabb's materialism explicit – Pip is quite clearly regarded as a valuable property to be exploited rather than as a human being.

Other characters who exemplify the futile and redundant lifestyle of the gentleman include the Finches, of whom the narrator remarks '[they] spent their money foolishly…' (Chapter 34, p.273). The most degenerate member of the Finches' club is, without doubt, Bentley Drummle. As we are informed in Chapter 23 (p.192), he is 'the next heir but one to a baronetcy'. The narrator also describes him as 'idle, proud, niggardly, reserved, and suspicious' (Chapter 25, p.203). Furthermore, he is 'Heavy in figure, movement, and comprehension…' and, as the narrator ironically remarks, '[he] took up a book as if its writer had done him an injury…' (Chapter 25, pp.202–03). His marriage to Estella is everything one would expect of such a dubious moral character.

Another character who Dickens uses to expose the contradiction that often exists between gentility of rank and gentility of nature, is the villainous Compeyson. Despite social status and education, Compeyson is the primary example of a villain in the novel and the one person most responsible, either directly or indirectly, for the various evils that beset most of the main characters. He jilts Miss Havisham on her wedding day, thus initiating her heartbreak and her obsessive desire for revenge on all men. This quite clearly has a major negative impact on the lives of both Pip and Estella. He also uses his knowledge of Magwitch's personal circumstances with regard to Molly and her supposed murder of their child in order to blackmail Magwitch into participating in his criminal schemes. When Herbert relates this aspect of Magwitch's history to Pip, he refers to 'That evil genius, Compeyson, the worst of scoundrels among many scoundrels…' (Chapter 50, p.407). It is also Compeyson who twice betrays Magwitch, the second occasion leading to Magwitch's recapture and ultimate death just as he is on the point of escaping the country (Chapter 54).

Education

It is clear from the above section on gentility that the education provided for the upper classes was often lacking in any real value. It certainly seems to have had no positive impact on either Compeyson or Drummle. Estella, also, has been sent 'Abroad … educating for a lady…' (Chapter 15, p.116). On her return many years later, all she seems to have learnt is how to ensnare men.

Another damning indictment of the education system provided for upper-class women is the example of Mrs Pocket, Matthew Pocket's hopelessly disorganised and inefficient wife. Her father was a knight and had her educated as befitted the family's elevated social position. It is clear that being socially useful or personally sufficient was not regarded as a relevant skill. Again, emphasis is placed primarily on such superficial features as appearance.

> **GRADE BOOSTER**
>
> ```
> You will help to improve your grade by demonstrating
> to your examiner an understanding that themes do not
> appear in isolation but instead are interwoven and
> often interconnected. The power of their combination is
> to reinforce the deeper meanings or the moral message
> of the novel.
> ```

Despite the dubious nature of the education provided for the privileged, Dickens makes it abundantly clear that, as far as the rich and powerful are concerned, a good education is to remain beyond the reach of the lower classes. As Pip the narrator comments in Chapter 12 (p.95), Miss Havisham '...seemed to prefer my being ignorant'. The reason for this, though not given at this point in the novel, is because education fosters talent and encourages a meritocracy, a society where people rise through ability, as opposed to an aristocracy, where those who hold power and wealth do so through no other reason than the good fortune of their birth. As Herbert explains to Pip in Chapter 22, Miss Havisham's father 'was a country gentleman down in your part of the world, and was a brewer' (p.180). Miss Havisham, however, who 'was a spoilt child' (p.180), has allowed the highly successful brewery business to fall idle and has entirely adopted the unproductive lifestyle that Dickens more regularly associated with her class. It is Joe who sums up the real power of education when, commenting on Mrs Joe, he remarks:

> 'And she an't over partial to having scholars on the premises,' Joe continued, 'and in partickler would not be over partial to my being a scholar, for fear as I might rise. Like a sort of rebel, don't you see?'
>
> (Chapter 7, p.49)

Consequently, the quality of education that is available to the poor is generally intentionally substandard. Certainly, both Joe and Magwitch are clear evidence of the lack of a worthwhile educational provision for those less well off.

Education is not just an isolated social theme that Dickens chooses to explore within the novel. It also becomes a key aspect of Pip's own character development. As a result of his first contact with Estella

Key quotation

Be that as it may, he had directed Mrs. Pocket to be brought up from her cradle as one who in the nature of things must marry a title, and who was to be guarded from the acquisition of plebeian domestic knowledge. So successful a watch and ward had been established over the young lady by this judicious parent, that she had grown up highly ornamental, but perfectly helpless and useless.

(Chapter 23, p.189)

Build critical skills

Read the description of the school run for the local children by Mr Wopsle's great-aunt in Chapter 10 (pp.73–74), which begins 'The Educational scheme or Course…' and ends '…one low-spirited dip-candle and no snuffers'. Consider the various ways in which Dickens presents this as being a poor quality of schooling.

and Miss Havisham, Pip perceives education as a means to upward social mobility, most likely reflecting Dickens' own social advancement through academic means. As Pip the narrator states at the beginning of Chapter 10:

> …I had a particular reason for wishing to get on in life, and that I should feel very much obliged to her if she would impart all her learning to me.

(p.73)

GRADE *BOOSTER*

An examiner will be impressed if you are able to demonstrate a brief and relevant understanding of how key events in a writer's life may have influenced his or her work if it is appropriate to the question. Read about the crucial importance of education in Dickens' own life on pages 9-10 of this guide.

Build critical skills

Having considered the importance of education within the novel, how does it make you feel about your own right to a free place in a state school? How might a modern reader's opinion on this subject differ from that of a Victorian reader?

Of course, once he is to become a gentleman, a more formal education is seen as essential. As Jaggers remarks when he informs Pip of his good fortune, 'It is considered that you must be better educated, in accordance with your altered position…' (Chapter 18, p.139). Admittedly, this education does have its frivolous aspects, as Herbert indicates when he explains, on Pip's first night in London, the vital importance of using a fork and not holding a spoon 'over-hand' (Chapter 22, p.179). Because Jaggers is a man of good sense, however, he ensures that Pip's London tutor, Matthew Pocket, is an able instructor. And, ultimately, it is not Pip's temporary existence as Magwitch's idle and artificially manufactured gentleman that secures his future, but his education, which enables him to become a productive and industrious partner in Clarriker's business, where 'we had a good name, and worked for our profits, and did very well' (Chapter 58, p.480).

Justice and mercy

In the novels of Charles Dickens, justice and mercy are crucially important themes that often drive the plot forward. Much of the sense of outrage and anger that Dickens communicates to the reader is created by a failure of natural justice on the part of the law and by an absence of mercy on the part of those who hold power.

In *Great Expectations*, as in many of Dickens' other works, the law is unjust and unequal, favouring the small, powerful and monied elite at the top of society. Admittedly, Jaggers is treated with great respect and Wemmick with an equal amount of affection. In Chapter 18, for example,

▲ Pip comforts the dying Magwitch in prison

Jaggers expounds upon the finer ideals of his profession when he demands of Wopsle whether or not he is aware of the fact that:

'...the law of England supposes every man to be innocent, until he is proved – proved – to be guilty?'

(p.134)

There is also, however, a wider world of legal indifference, incompetence and corruption that prevails just beyond Jaggers' office. The young Pip is aware of the law as a tool of oppression of the lower classes. After his impromptu boxing bout with the youthful Herbert Pocket, his thoughts are conveyed as:

...the Law would avenge it. Without having any definite idea of the penalties I had incurred, it was clear to me that village boys could not go stalking about the country, ravaging the houses of gentlefolks and pitching into the studious youth of England, without laying themselves open to severe punishment.

(Chapter 12, pp.93–94)

Build critical skills

Think about how Dickens uses the themes of justice and mercy as a plot device. Find three examples where he uses them to deepen the reader's emotional attachment to his heroes and heroines, while simultaneously critiquing one of the great evils of his society.

But the person who most suffers as a result of the class discrimination at the heart of the legal system is, of course, Magwitch. Shortly after his revelation that he is Pip's benefactor, he relates the events that caused him to become the escaped convict whom Pip helped on the momentous day described at the opening of the novel. Both Magwitch and Compeyson had been arrested for 'a charge of putting stolen notes in circulation...' (Chapter 42, p.350), which today would be termed money-laundering. Although Magwitch was the junior partner in the crime, he was given the lion's share of the sentence. Magwitch explains:

> 'And when it come to character, warn't it Compeyson as had been to the school, and warn't it his schoolfellows as was in this position and in that, and warn't it him as had been know'd by witnesses in such clubs and societies, and nowt to his disadvantage?'
>
> (Chapter 42, p.351)

The heavily biased and unfair verdict is that Compeyson receives a sentence of seven years whereas Magwitch's term is set at fourteen years. The tragic conclusion to Magwitch's role within the novel again points out the heartlessness of the system. The judge sentences Magwitch to hang rather than mercifully delaying the sentence so that he can be left to die of his injuries. The brutality of the system is also highlighted by the fact that on the day appointed for Magwitch's execution, he is just one of a total of 'two-and-thirty men and women' sentenced to die (Chapter 56, p.457).

Romantic love

Great Expectations is one of Dickens' most romantic novels, most likely because of his then-current relationship with the young actress Ellen Ternan (see p.10 of this guide). As well as being a major theme, Pip's unrequited love for Estella is essential to the overall structure of the novel as it helps to drive the plot forward. As in all romances, the main source of suspense is the reader's curiosity as to how, and even *if*, the problem that separates the potential lovers will be resolved.

In the original ending to the novel, Dickens had Estella marry a 'Shropshire doctor' after the death of Drummle. Before publication, Dickens showed this ending to Sir Edward Bulwer-Lytton, a friend and fellow novelist, who strongly urged him to write a more positive conclusion so as not to disappoint the reader. On the basis of this advice, Dickens decided to change the ending to what we now have, a strong implication of a marriage between Pip and Estella some time after the novel ends.

A perfect example of ideal romantic love within the novel is Herbert Pocket's relationship with Clara Barley. It is never sufficiently developed to be termed a subplot, but it does act as a dramatic contrast to Pip's relationship with Estella and allows Dickens to offer observations concerning the true nature of romantic love. Herbert intends to marry Clara regardless of the fact that 'she is rather below my mother's nonsensical family notions' (Chapter 30, p.252). It is her character and not her social status that is her defining quality. Pip the narrator later describes her as having 'something so confiding, loving, and innocent, in her modest manner of yielding herself to Herbert's embracing arm...' (Chapter 46, p.376). Estella, by contrast, is incapable of love at this time in her life due to Miss Havisham's training, and so Herbert's match with Clara starkly contrasts with Estella's own socially desirable but essentially frigid and violent union with Drummle.

The darker side of romantic love is explored through Miss Havisham. Her definition of love is savagely imparted to Pip when he visits Satis House on Estella's return from her foreign education:

> 'I'll tell you,' said she, in the same hurried passionate whisper, 'what real love is. It is blind devotion, unquestioning self-humiliation, utter submission, trust and belief against yourself and against the whole world, giving up your whole heart and soul to the smiter – as I did!'
>
> (Chapter 29, p.240)

In many respects, this mirrors Pip's own obsessive and unrequited feelings for Estella. The main clue to the distinctive feature that distinguishes Pip's infatuation from Miss Havisham's, however, is the use of the word 'smiter', which clearly indicates that her passion also embodies a powerful sense of accusation and hatred.

GRADE BOOSTER

```
Notice how many themes Miss Havisham encompasses:
vengeance, unrequited love, upper-class indolence,
adult corruption of youth, et cetera. She is an
excellent example of how themes are interconnected and
of how theme and character are often indivisible.
```

Forgiveness and redemption

In opposition to the increasingly secular mood of the times (see pp.11–12 of this guide), it is clear that Dickens writes from a broadly Christian point of view when exploring themes through his characters and plots. Towards the end of Chapter 56 (p.458), for example, the narrator refers to 'the greater Judgment that knoweth all things and cannot err'. Forgiveness and redemption are two Christian virtues that certainly feature in *Great Expectations*.

The novel undoubtedly incorporates characters who are beyond redemption. True villains, such as Drummle, Orlick and Compeyson, never waver from their downward path and so earn no sympathy from the reader. A number of other characters – including, of course, Pip and Magwitch – however, do ultimately appreciate the errors of their ways and seek to reform. This is generally associated with a strong desire for forgiveness.

The moral epiphany (awakening) comes late for characters such as Miss Havisham, Mrs Joe and Arthur (Miss Havisham's deceitful half-brother) and, therefore, they are unable to reap the kind of spiritual and psychological benefits of living with a clear conscience that enrich Pip's life in the latter stages of the novel. All three of the above characters, however, obtain a degree of enlightenment shortly before their deaths. The severely disabled Mrs Joe, for example, seeks Pip's forgiveness for the harsh and unloving regime of punishment that she inflicted on him when he was a child, her last words being 'Pardon' and 'Pip' (Chapter 35, p.283).

A much more significant exploration of these themes occurs via Miss Havisham. Her first pangs of conscience arise just before Estella drops the bombshell that she is to marry Drummle. When Miss Havisham suddenly perceives the degree of heartbreak that she has wilfully inflicted on Pip, the narrator describes seeing her 'put her hand to her heart and hold it there...' (Chapter 44, p.362). One of the most compelling examples of both forgiveness and redemption within the entire novel occurs several chapters later between the same two characters:

> 'My name is on the first leaf. If you can ever write under my name, "I forgive her," though ever so long after my broken heart is dust – pray do it!'

> 'O Miss Havisham,' said I, 'I can do it now. There have been sore mistakes; and my life has been a blind and thankless one; and I want forgiveness and direction far too much, to be bitter with you.'
>
> (Chapter 49, p.398)

It is clear from this section of their dialogue that personal reflection and self-awareness are essential prerequisites for forgiveness, which is probably why other characters make no moral improvement. Compeyson regrets nothing, including his cruel deception of Miss Havisham, but the awareness of responsibility for his role in the ruin of Miss Havisham's life haunts her half-brother Arthur to the very end. He dies as a hopeless alcoholic, haunted by a vision of a heartbroken Miss Havisham.

Build critical skills

Re-read Chapters 49 and 57 and think about why Miss Havisham desperately seeks forgiveness from Pip and why Pip is so full of regret for his past behaviour towards Joe. What does this powerful sense of shame reveal to us about the moral growth of both of these characters?

GRADE *FOCUS*

Grade 5

To achieve Grade 5, students should reveal a clear understanding of the novel's key themes and how Dickens' use of language, form and structure explores these, supported by close reference to the text.

Grade 8

To achieve Grade 8, students will be able to examine and evaluate the novel's key themes, analysing the ways that Dickens uses language, form and structure to explore them. Comments will be supported by carefully chosen, integrated references to the text.

REVIEW YOUR LEARNING

(Answers are given on p.101.)

1   Which themes have been identified in this section of the guide?

2   What can we learn about Victorian society from Dickens' treatment of the themes highlighted in this section of the guide?

3   Which of these themes help Dickens to create his characters and develop his plot?

4   Which themes are most closely associated with Dickens' own personal experiences?

5   Whom does Pip show mercy to towards the end of the novel?

6   Whom does Pip seek forgiveness from, and why?

7   Which characters are most identified with the theme of remorse immediately prior to their deaths?

8   How does Dickens want the reader ultimately to feel about these characters?

Language, style and analysis

Target your thinking

- What features does the term 'style' refer to? (**AO2**)
- What viewpoint does Charles Dickens adopt? (**AO2**)
- What is characteristic about Dickens' style? (**AO2**)
- How does Dickens create humour? (**AO2**)
- How does Dickens use settings in order to develop major themes? (**AO2**)
- In what ways does Dickens use imagery? (**AO2**)

A definition of style

When responding on an aspect of Dickens' style you should first define your terms, i.e. explain to the examiner that you understand what this phrase means in relation to this novel. A novelist's style is his or her distinctive manner of writing, i.e. what makes his or her writing unique. A writer's style may develop and change over time but will nevertheless retain characteristic features that a regular reader of that author will come to recognise.

Dickens has a distinctive style that makes his writing different from most of the novels that we would read today. His writing is also different from that of many of the authors of his own day, such as Thomas Hardy, George Eliot and Elizabeth Gaskell. They tended to create characters and situations that closely resembled reality and, therefore, their style is naturalistic. Dickens also commented on real life, but tended to exaggerate characters and situations for either comic or tragic effect.

GRADE BOOSTER

Demonstrating an appreciation of an author's style is a sophisticated skill and exam questions are unlikely to address this aspect alone. Remember, however, that all the exam boards require you to consider the way the writer uses language, structure and form to create effects. (AO2)

Narrative viewpoint

The first-person narrator

A major consideration when analysing style is the position from which the author writes the story. *Great Expectations* is related from the first-person narrative point of view ('I'), and the reader is intended to assume that the story is being told by Pip, the main character in the novel. All the perceptions and judgements in the novel are presented as being from Pip's point of view and, just as he is one of many characters in the novel, his version of the 'truth' is just one of many possible versions.

Dickens' mocking narrative tone

'Tone' refers to the emotional feel of the writing, for example comic, sad, angry or ironic. The tone may also be a more sophisticated combination of a number of emotions. Although *Great Expectations* is presented via a first-person narrator (Pip), much of its tone is that of the acerbic voice of Dickens himself. The bitingly ironic and often cynical voice is one of the predominant characteristics of his style, whether the novel be in the first person or in the god-like, all-knowing, omniscient third-person narrative style. It is the voice of an often-judgemental narrator who cannot resist the urge to lampoon his own creations for comic effect. Even some of Dickens' most admirable characters cannot escape this heavily mocking commentary of riotous slapstick humour and are often treated in a most undignified manner.

> **GRADE BOOSTER**
>
> ```
> Understanding the difference between a first- and a
> third-person narrator is a useful skill. A third-person
> narrator is all-seeing and all-knowing. A first-person
> narrator is much more limited, being able to see things
> from only one perspective.
> ```

> **GRADE BOOSTER**
>
> ```
> In your examination response, you will score well for
> including such perceptive analysis as highlighting the
> differences in Dickens' narrative tone and explaining
> their effects.
> ```

Build critical skills

In order to appreciate how unreliable a first-person narrator can be, ask yourself how much sympathy there would have been for Pip in the early chapters of the novel if the narrative had been relayed through Mrs Joe.

Lampoon: to make fun of, to ridicule, to send-up.

Irony

The meaning of 'ironic', as it has been used above, is similar to sarcastic, but irony is a much higher form of wit. It is when the literal sense of the writing suggests one thing, but the context of the situation tells the reader that the writer's meaning is the opposite of what the literal meaning would suggest. Dickens regularly uses this technique. So, for example, on Joe's first visit to Pip in London, the narrator compliments Joe on his ability to return his hat to his head by describing his actions as requiring 'a constant attention, and a quickness of eye and hand, very like that exacted by wicket-keeping' (Chapter 27, p.222). It might initially appear as if the narrator is actually praising Joe's skilfulness. In reality, the writing is ironic because the narrator is pointing out how awkward and clumsy Joe is, so much so that he cannot even keep his hat on his head.

Authorial intrusion

On occasions, Dickens actually has the narrator acknowledge the mismatch between the innate moral goodness of a character and the ruthless way in which the narrator/Dickens has ridiculed that same character in order to create humour.

As we have seen, the narrator makes extensive fun of Joe's manners, speech and clothing during his first London visit. But this disrespectful presentation creates a disparity with the high moral value that the narrator wishes to place on Joe. Dickens tries to lessen this gap by having the narrator remark:

> Joe looked at me for a single instant with something faintly like reproach. Utterly preposterous as his cravat was, and as his collars were, I was conscious of a sort of dignity in the look.
>
> (Chapter 27, p.222)

It could be argued, of course, that Pip's often disrespectful narrative tone is simply symptomatic of the character's own immaturity at this stage in the novel. But the narrative is actually told by the mature Pip reflecting upon past events, and this mature narrator, unlike his younger self, is quite able to see that Joe's extreme awkwardness 'was all my fault' (p.222). It is also worth mentioning that the narrator's heavily ironic and comically exaggerated treatment of Joe occurs from the beginning of the novel – before Pip has even met Miss Havisham and Estella, which is the point when Pip first becomes ashamed of Joe's simple rustic ways. Furthermore, the same tone is used for many other characters within the novel and, more importantly, can be heard throughout every Dickens novel – which is why it is fair to say that it is an essential aspect of Dickens' style rather than a specific quality belonging to Pip as narrator.

Another good example of the narrative voice consciously acknowledging that the lampooning of an admirable character may have gone too far is with regard to Matthew Pocket. Matthew Pocket, Herbert Pocket's father and Pip's London tutor, is generally acknowledged to be a person of high moral worth. Even Estella tells Pip how she has heard that 'he really is disinterested, and above small jealousy and spite' (Chapter 33, p.266). And yet the narrative voice grossly ridicules his management of his own household, which is depicted as being comically disorganised to an unbelievable degree. Ultimately, in order to restore some semblance of dignity to the worthwhile Matthew, Dickens has the narrator remark: 'Nor, did I ever regard him as having anything ludicrous about him – or anything but what was serious, honest, and good – in his tutor communication with me' (Chapter 24, p.197).

You could re-read all of Chapter 23 and consider the various ways in which Matthew Pocket, a classic stock comic character, is comically frustrated by his wife's behaviour. Also consider the various amusing ways in which Dickens portrays this frustration, for example his increasingly desperate hair pulling, as the chapter progresses.

> **Build critical skills**
>
> Read the description of Joe on page 222 (Chapter 27), from 'I really believe Joe would have prolonged this word…' to '…heaped coals of fire on my head'. How does Dickens make Joe seem ridiculous in order to amuse the reader? Look particularly at the way Dickens exaggerates the awkwardness of his speech, actions and dress.

Exceptions to the rule

There are, however, a number of characters who are either rarely or never subjected to the narrator's intense comic ridicule. These are the more serious characters within the novel, including Miss Havisham, Estella, Biddy, Bentley Drummle, Orlick and Compeyson. Their speech and behaviour is devoid of the kind of comic eccentricities explored above. When Orlick threatens violence, for example, it is no laughing matter, as in Chapter 53 when he intends to murder Pip with a stone-hammer and then dispose of his remains in a lime-kiln.

The self-ridiculing satirical narrator

It is worth noting that Pip the character is also ridiculed by Pip the narrator. On these occasions the bitingly ironic tone has more of a satirical purpose, that being to show how pompous and ridiculous Pip has become as a result of his new-found status as a gentleman. An excellent example of this is the narrator's use of Trabb's boy, particularly

> **GRADE BOOSTER**
>
> Lampoonery is another characteristic feature of Dickens' style and the examiner will be impressed if you can apply the term relevantly.

> **Build critical skills**
>
> Read the passage on page 196 (Chapter 23) beginning with the housemaid saying 'Begging your pardon, ma'am' and continuing to the end of that chapter. Note down examples of typical Dickensian exaggeration of a character's weaknesses, for example Mrs Pocket's inability to understand the extent of the mayhem all around her.

Satirical: a style of writing that makes a moral point by poking fun at the vice or foolishness of someone or something.

in Chapter 30. Although only a minor character and of a low social status himself, the boy is able to see the ludicrous nature of Pip's snobbish behaviour. Therefore, he provides a stark contrast to Trabb, and the other local businessmen, who are falling over themselves to take Pip seriously because all they can see is money and rank.

The romantic narrative voice

There is, however, a different kind of narrative voice that surfaces significantly on occasions. Although still obviously an aspect of Dickens' style (as it is he, not Pip, who has actually written the novel), this voice could be regarded as the authentic voice of Pip, the character who both appears in the novel and narrates the story. In Chapter 30, while discussing Pip's relations with Estella, Herbert describes Pip as 'a boy whom nature and circumstances made so romantic...' (p.250). When the narrative voice also becomes so romantic that it no longer embodies Dickens' characteristic sermonising or mocking tone, then this could be viewed as Pip, the character, speaking rather than Dickens.

For a perfect example of the romantic tone of Pip's narrative voice see Chapter 44, in which Pip recounts the horror and dismay he feels when his beloved Estella informs him that she is to marry the heartless and insensitive Bentley Drummle.

This can be compared with the opening page of Chapter 45, when Pip has to stay overnight in a rundown hotel. The comic narrative voice returns here with a sudden vengeance, this time lampooning the furniture. The bedroom, for example, is described as having 'a despotic monster of a four-post bedstead in it...' (p.366). Other aspects of this room are also presented in an amusing and ironic way.

Humour

Slapstick humour

Slapstick humour is associated with physical action of a boisterous and often ridiculous nature, and is a Dickensian stylistic feature. Much slapstick humour is created through the use of random acts of violence, talk about random acts of violence or the desire to commit such acts of violence. Dickens is able to turn what would be horrific in reality into amusement for the reader because of his use of caricature. In this respect his style is similar to such children's cartoons as *Bugs Bunny* and *Tom and Jerry* in which the most extreme act, such as blowing somebody up or dropping them off a cliff, is funny because there is no real harm done and any pain experienced is moderate and short lived. In Dickens' time, a comparable form of entertainment would have been the Punch and Judy puppet shows.

An early example of this stylistic feature occurs in Chapter 2, when Mrs Joe makes a variety of physical assaults on both the seven-year-old Pip and the adult Joe:

> By this time, my sister was quite desperate, so she pounced on Joe, and, taking him by the two whiskers, knocked his head for a little while against the wall behind him...

(pp.11–12)

In the same chapter, Pip and Joe are both dosed with tar-water (a vile-tasting concoction of tar and water, generally used as a disinfectant) and Pip is savagely lashed with Tickler and then hurled as 'a connubial missile' (p.9) at the hapless Joe.

Although fundamentally a gentle and good-natured character, even Pip is not immune from the desire to commit cartoon violence, as is demonstrated in Chapter 43 (p.356), when Pip the narrator reveals that his 23-year-old self would like to take Bentley Drummle in his arms 'and seat him on the fire'.

Other comic techniques

Dickens also creates comedy through his use of such techniques as incongruity, juxtaposition, eccentric dialogue or behaviour, puns and exaggeration. The comedy often arises from the combination of any number of these techniques. The impact can be particularly hilarious when he includes slapstick humour as well.

> **GRADE BOOSTER**
>
> When analysing a comic passage from *Great Expectations*, always try to point out and explain the stylistic features that Dickens uses to signal humour to the reader. This will ensure you pin down how the humour is created.

An excellent example of all aspects of Dickens' comic technique comes in the Christmas dinner scene in Chapter 4. Notice the following:

- The behaviour of most of the adults is incongruous (inappropriate). They are spiteful towards Pip on an occasion that should reflect the season of goodwill.
- Pumblechook, in particular, is ludicrous (ridiculously eccentric). For example, he verbally attacks Pip by comparing him to a pig to be slaughtered by 'Dunstable the butcher' (p.27).
- There is an example of juxtaposition when 'the Pumblechookian elbow [was] in my eye' (p.25). Juxtaposition is the placing in close proximity of unrelated things, which can then create humour through the inappropriateness of their connection.

Build critical skills

Think about why a modern audience, which is so very attuned to such issues as domestic abuse, might find these passages much less appealing than the readers of Dickens' day.

Build critical skills

If these acts of violence were instead treated realistically by the narrator, Chapter 2 would constitute a case of severe child abuse. How would that affect the tone of the novel? (See 'Answers' section.)

- There is use of a pun (a double meaning) when Pumblechook tells Pip that Mrs Joe 'brought you up by hand' (p.26). Pumblechook is using the phrase to imply that Mrs Joe's touch is caring and maternal, but the reader knows that her touch is that of frequent and unprovoked bouts of violence.

- An excellent example of slapstick humour occurs when the pompous Pumblechook drinks the adulterated brandy and displays exaggerated symptoms of distress: 'violently plunging and expectorating, making the most hideous faces, and apparently out of his mind' (p.28).

> **GRADE BOOSTER**
>
> The examiner will be impressed if you respond to a question that enables you to comment on Dickens' creation of humour by using and showing an understanding of such sophisticated vocabulary as 'incongruity', 'juxtaposition', 'ludicrous', 'irony' and 'pun'.

Settings and symbolism

As you read this section, notice how settings are not just used to set the scene but are also frequently used to symbolise much bigger ideas, such as the harshness of Pip's life, the frequent cruelty of humankind or the moral shortcomings of society.

The marshes

Dickens sometimes uses landscape and setting in order to represent the harshness of life. The most comprehensive way in which this meaning is conveyed in *Great Expectations* is through the depiction of the marshes that surround Pip's village. Outside Joe's forge and just beyond his warm hearth is a world of seemingly perpetual cold and mist. On the opening page of Chapter 1, the narrator immediately sets the scene when he refers to 'a memorable raw afternoon' and 'a bleak place overgrown with nettles', meaning the churchyard. The reader is introduced to an inhospitable world in which nature is both hostile and threatening. The sense of menace is further enhanced by the fact that the location is a graveyard and, judging from the high number of Pip's deceased relatives, it is a world in which death is more prevalent than life.

The sense of an antagonistic and dangerous world is further reinforced by the reference to 'a gibbet with some chains hanging to it which had once held a pirate' (Chapter 1, p.7). A gibbet is a gallows and clearly the pirate had been publicly hanged upon it. In Chapter 5, to further reinforce the point, the narrator uses pathetic fallacy and states 'the weather was cold and threatening' (p.34). Also in Chapter 5, the narrator employs personification when he refers to 'the low red glare of sunset' (p.35), thus conveying a universal sense of anger. Taken altogether, we are presented with a vision of nettles, weeds and wilderness, with booming cannons and escaped convicts shackled and frozen. The nightmare scenario is made all the more terrifying in that it is viewed through the eyes of a frightened child.

The black hulk

Perhaps the most menacing image of all is the description of the prison ship to which Magwitch and Compeyson are being returned.

This simile compares the prison ship to Noah's ark. In the Bible, God orders Noah to build an ark and rescue his family from the coming flood that will rid the world of the sinful aspects of humanity. Dickens here, however, uses the ark as a symbol of the survival of evil rather than its destruction, and the clear cleansing water of God's flood has become an unclean morass of mud. He refers again to 'the wicked Noah's Ark lying out on the black water' in Chapter 28 (p.230). Once more, the water seems impure and the adjective 'black' conveys a powerful sense of evil.

Mist

The most significant symbol of the moral blindness of man occurs through the narrator's frequent references to the marshes being covered by mist. Mist also reflects the mistaken paths stumbled upon by such characters as Pip, Magwitch and Miss Havisham, all of whom are deceived by others and so 'lose their way'. In the first reference to the mist, the narrator explicitly makes a connection between physical and moral blindness.

The post showing the direction of the village is initially obscured. When Pip does locate it, the thick mist makes it appear like a ghostly finger pointing the way not so much towards the village as to the prison ships, the predominant image of evil in this early part of the novel:

> On every rail and gate, wet lay clammy; and the marsh-mist was so thick, that the wooden finger on the post directing people to our village ... was invisible to me until I was quite close under it. Then, as I looked up at it, while it dripped, it seemed to my oppressed conscience like a phantom devoting me to the Hulks.
>
> (Chapter 3, pp.16–17)

This impression of a fallen world contrasts starkly with the time of year. The opening chapters take place on Christmas Eve and Christmas Day. As in Dickens' famous story *A Christmas Carol*, the timing is deliberate. It is the season when the selfless example of Christ should be foremost in people's minds, yet there is little love or compassion to be found in the young Pip's world.

Key quotation

...the black Hulk lying out a little way from the mud of the shore, like a wicked Noah's ark.

(Chapter 5, p.40)

GRADE BOOSTER

```
Notice the
deliberate
reference to
Dickens' use
of simile in
the explanation
of the Noah's
ark image.
Examiners
love to read
explanations
that exhibit
this level of
sophistication.
```

GRADE BOOSTER

```
Pathetic
fallacy and
personification
are similar, as
personification
can also be
used to give
human qualities
to nature. Make
sure that you
are able to use
both terms with
confidence.
```

London

The other great 'fallen' world depicted in the novel is that of London. Pip's first impression is that it is 'rather ugly, crooked, narrow and dirty' (Chapter 20, p.163). Just as 'mist' pervades the marshes, dirt is a recurring motif in London. Wemmick sums up the moral calibre of both London and the age in general when he tells Pip:

> 'You may get cheated, robbed and murdered, in London. But there are plenty of people anywhere, who'll do that for you.'
>
> (Chapter 21, p.172)

And, once again, a death image is quickly introduced:

> We entered this haven through a wicket-gate, and were disgorged by an introductory passage into a melancholy little square that looked to me like a flat burying-ground. I thought it had the most dismal trees in it, and the most dismal sparrows, and the most dismal cats, and the most dismal houses (in number half a dozen or so), that I had ever seen.
>
> (Chapter 21, p.173)

Motif: a recurring object or idea in a text or work of art.

Notice the repetition of the adjective 'dismal', another frequently used word in the novel. It suggests a general absence of vitality and life.

Build critical skills

Read the full description of Barnard's Inn in Chapter 21 (p.173), beginning 'We entered this haven' and ending '"Try Barnard's mixture"'. Note the ironic use of the word 'haven'. See how many references you can find to death, dirt and decay.

▲ Victorian slums depicted by Gustave Doré

Dickens' use of imagery

As you can see from the above analysis of Dickens' style, he is a writer who relies heavily on figurative language – that is, language that contains a high density of poetic features such as similes, metaphors, personifications and symbols. Often these images form part of an overall pattern that helps Dickens to create a particular atmosphere or to make a particular moral point. As we have already seen, Dickens uses places in this way. He also likes to reveal character through imagery. Mrs Joe, for example, is initially associated with objects that could cause pain: pins, needles, a knife, a nutmeg-grater.

Dickens does not persist in the use of this particular symbolic tag much beyond Chapter 2, but other characters are characterised by a use of imagery that follows them throughout the entire novel. Wemmick, Jaggers' clerk, is a good example of this, his associated image being that his mouth often resembles a 'post-office' (for example, Chapter 25, p. 210). This suggests the tightening of his mouth into a narrow slit once he resumes his city persona. Another example is the extended metaphor of a castle to characterise Wemmick's house. Presumably this symbolises how his home enables him to escape his tense city personality and become the loving son of an 'aged parent'.

GRADE BOOSTER

An extended metaphor is a metaphor that is built up over several lines, paragraphs, or sometimes even longer sections of the text. This is another useful term that you could exemplify and comment upon in your exam responses.

Whether extended or not, imagery is one of the most powerful tools Dickens uses in order to communicate with his reader and make his writing vivid (visual). Take, for example, this description of Pip's despair when he discovers that his real patron is Magwitch and not Miss Havisham after all: 'it was not until I began to think, that I began fully to know how wrecked I was, and how the ship in which I had sailed was gone to pieces' (Chapter 39, p.323). While you are reading through the novel, look out for imagery being used just as this metaphor has been used, simply to create a poetic picture in the reader's mind.

Build critical skills

Read the first description of Wemmick's home in Chapter 25, pages 206–07, and see how many humorous castle references you can find. Note how the comedy arises from the contrast between the humble reality of Wemmick's wooden cottage and his vision of it as a medieval fortress.

GRADE *FOCUS*

Grade 5

To achieve Grade 5, students will show a clear appreciation of the methods Dickens uses to create effects for the reader, supported by appropriate references to the novel.

Grade 8

To achieve Grade 8, students will explore and analyse the methods that Dickens uses to create effects for the reader, supported by carefully chosen and well-integrated references to the novel.

REVIEW YOUR LEARNING

(Answers are given on p.101.)

1   How would you define the term 'a writer's style'?

2   What is distinctive about Dickens' use of the narrative voice in *Great Expectations*?

3   How does Dickens make use of places in *Great Expectations*?

4   What different techniques does Dickens use in order to create humour?

5   How is Dickens' presentation of Miss Havisham, Estella and Biddy different from his presentation of Mrs Joe or Pumblechook, and why do you think this might be?

6   Why does Dickens not use cartoon violence in his presentation of Orlick?

7   How would you describe figurative language?

8   What is a motif?

Tackling the examination questions

Target your thinking

- What sorts of questions will you have to answer in the exam?
- What is the best way to plan your answer?
- How might you improve your grade?
- What do you have to do to achieve the highest grade?

Your response to a question on *Great Expectations* will be assessed in a 'closed book' English literature examination, which means that you are not allowed to take copies of the text into the examination room. Different examination boards will test you in different ways and it is vital that you know on which paper the nineteenth-century novel will be so that you can be well-prepared on the day of the examination.

Whichever board you are studying, the table on page 66 explains in which paper and section the novel appears and gives you information about the sort of question you will face and how you will be assessed.

Marking

The marking of your responses will vary according to the exam board your school or you have chosen. Each exam board will have a slightly different mark scheme, consisting of a ladder of levels. The marks you achieve in each part of the examination will be converted to your final overall grade. Grades are numbered from 1 to 9, with 9 being the highest.

It is important that you familiarise yourself with the relevant mark scheme(s) for your examination. After all, how can you do well unless you know exactly what is required?

Assessment Objectives for individual assessments are explained in the next section of the guide (see p.74).

Approaching the examination question

First impressions

First, read the whole question and make sure you understand *exactly* what the task requires you to do. It is very easy in the highly pressured atmosphere of the examination room to misread a question – and this can be disastrous. Under no circumstances should you try and twist the

Exam board	AQA	Edexcel	OCR
Paper and section	Paper 1 Section B	Paper 2 Section A	Paper 1 Section B
Type of question	Extract-based question requiring response to an aspect of the extract and response to the same or similar aspect in the novel as a whole.	Two-part question: • Part A is based on an extract. • Part B asks for a response to an aspect elsewhere in the text.	Extract-based question requiring response to an aspect of the extract and response to the same or similar aspect elsewhere in the novel. **Or:** Question requiring the exploration of character, theme (or possibly stylistic aspect) in 'at least two moments from the novel'.
Closed book?	Yes	Yes	Yes
Choice of question?	No	No	Yes
Paper and section length	Paper 1 = 1 hour 45 minutes Section B = approx.. 50 minutes	Paper 2 = 2 hours 15 minutes Section A = 55 minutes	Paper = 2 hours Section B = 45 minutes
Percentage of whole grade	20% of Literature grade	25% of Literature grade	25% of Literature grade
AOs assessed	AO1 AO2 AO3	Part A: AO2 Part B: AO1	AO1 AO2 AO3 AO4
Is AO4 (SPaG) assessed?	No	No	Yes

question to the one that you have spent hours revising or the one that you did brilliantly on in your mock exam!

Are you being asked to think about how a character or theme is being presented, or is it a description of a place? Make sure you know so that you will be able to sustain your focus later.

Look carefully at any bullet points you are given. They are there to help and guide you.

The three boards that offer *Great Expectations* as a text all use an extract-based question. The wordings and formats of the questions, however, are slightly different.

AQA

A typical AQA character question looks like this:

Starting with this extract, how does Dickens present Miss Havisham as a deeply psychologically disturbed character?

Write about:

⬤ how Dickens presents Miss Havisham in this extract

⬤ how Dickens presents Miss Havisham in the novel as a whole.

(Extract taken from Chapter 8, pp.57–58: 'She was dressed in rich materials…').

A typical AQA thematic question looks like this:

Starting with this extract, write about how Dickens presents the damaging effect of revenge within the world of the novel.

Write about:

⬤ how Dickens presents Magwitch's thirst for revenge in this extract

⬤ how Dickens presents the damaging impact of revenge in the novel as a whole.

(Extract taken from Chapter 39, pp.321–22: 'They shall be yourn, dear boy, if money can buy 'em…').

Edexcel

A typical Edexcel character question looks like this:

a   Explore how Dickens presents Pip's thoughts and feelings about Joe in this extract.

Give examples from the extract to support your ideas.

b   In this extract, Pip's early life is shown.

Explain the change in Pip's attitude towards Joe elsewhere in the novel.

In your answer you must consider:

⬤ why Pip behaves towards Joe in the various ways that he does

⬤ what this reveals about Pip's character.

(Extract taken from Chapter 14, p.107: 'How much of my ungracious condition of mind may have been my own fault…').

A typical Edexcel thematic/stylistic question looks like this:

a   Explore how Dickens presents Victorian London in this extract. Give examples from the extract to support your ideas.

b   In this extract, a powerful impression of Victorian London is created. Explain why the setting is important elsewhere in the novel.

In your answer you must consider:
* the different locations
* why they are important.

(Extract taken from Chapter 21, p.173: 'We entered this haven through a wicket-gate…').

OCR

A typical OCR character question looks like this:

Explore how Dickens presents ideas about what makes a good person through the presentation of Biddy in this extract and elsewhere in the novel.

(Extract taken from Chapter 19, pp.149–50: '"Oh! there are many kinds of pride," said Biddy…').

A typical OCR thematic question looks like this:

'Other characters' desire for revenge is the source of all Pip's problems.' How far do you agree with this view? Explore at least two moments from the novel to support your ideas.

Note that this question refers to 'two moments from the novel' rather than to a specific extract and 'elsewhere in the novel'.

Important: All three boards assess both AO1 and AO2 in this section of the paper. Always make sure you cover both of these AOs in your response, even if they do not seem to be signposted clearly in the question!

Whichever exam board you are using, you will be required to read a passage, so your next step is to **read the passage very carefully**, trying to get an overview or general impression of what is going on, and what or who is being described.

'Working with' the text

Now **read the passage again**, underlining or highlighting any words or short phrases that you think are related to the focus of the question and are of special interest. For example, they might be surprising, unusual or amusing. You might have a strong emotional or analytical reaction to them, or you might think that they are particularly clever or noteworthy.

These words/phrases may work together to produce a particular effect, or to get you to think about a particular theme or to explore the methods the writer uses to present a character in a particular way for their own purposes. You may pick out examples of literary techniques such as lists or use of imagery, or sound effects such as alliteration or onomatopoeia. You may spot an unusual word order, sentence construction or use of punctuation. The important thing to remember is that when you start writing you must try to **explain the effects** created by these words/phrases or techniques, and not simply identify what they mean. Above all, ensure that you are answering the question.

Planning your answer

It is advisable to write a brief plan before you start writing your response, in order to avoid repeating yourself or getting into a muddle. A plan is not a first draft. You will not have time to do this. In fact, if your plan consists of full sentences at all, you are probably eating into the time you have available for writing a really insightful and considered answer.

A plan is important, however, because it helps you to gather and organise your thoughts – but it should consist of only brief words and phrases.

You may find it helpful to use a diagram of some sort – perhaps a **spider diagram** or **flow chart**. This may help you to keep your mind open to new ideas as you plan, so that you can slot them in. Or you could make a list instead. The important thing is to choose a method that works for you.

If you have made a spider diagram, arranging your thoughts is a simple matter of numbering the branches in the best possible order.

The other advantage of having a plan is that if you run out of time, the examiner can look at the plan and may be able to give you an extra mark or two based on what you had planned to do next.

Writing your answer

And they're off...

Now you are ready to start writing your answer. The first thing to remember is that you are working against the clock and so it's really important to use your time wisely.

It is possible that you may not have time to deal with all of the points you wish to make in your response. If you simply identify several language features and make a brief comment on each, you will be working at a fairly low level. The idea is to **select** the ones that you find most interesting and develop them in a sustained and detailed manner. In order to move up the levels in the mark scheme, it is important to write a lot about a little, rather than a little about a lot.

You must also remember to address the whole question as you will be penalised if you fail to do so.

If you have any time left at the end of the examination, do not waste it! Check carefully that your meaning is clear and that you have done the very best that you can. Look back at your plan and check that you have included all your best points. Is there anything else you can add? Keep thinking until you are told to put your pen down!

Referring to the author and title

You can refer to Dickens either by name (make sure you spell it correctly) or as 'the writer'. You should never use his first name (Charles) – this sounds as if you know him personally. You can also save time by giving the novel title in full the first time you refer to it, and afterwards simply referring to it as 'the novel'.

When explaining how Dickens' message is conveyed to you, for instance through an event or a character, or through the use of symbolism, personification, irony, etc., don't forget to mention Dickens by name.

For example:

- Dickens makes it clear that...

- It is evident from ... that Dickens is inviting the audience to consider...

- Here, the audience may well feel that Dickens is suggesting...

Writing in an appropriate style

Remember that you are expected to write in a suitable **register**, i.e. that you need to use an **appropriate** style. This means:

- *not* using colloquial language or slang, for example, 'Compeyson is a nasty piece of work. A bit of a toe-rag really.' (The only exception is when quoting from the text.)

- *not* becoming too personal, for example, 'Joe is like my mate, right, 'cos he...'

- using suitable phrases for an academic essay, for example, 'It could be argued that...', *not* 'I reckon that...'

- *not* being too dogmatic: don't say 'This means that...'; it is much better to say, 'This might suggest that...'.

You are also expected to be able to use a range of technical terms correctly. If you can't remember the correct name for a technique but can describe its effect, you should still go ahead and do so.

GRADE BOOSTER

Do not lose sight of the author in your essay. Remember that the novel is a construct - the characters, their thoughts, their words and their actions have all been created by Dickens.

GRADE BOOSTER

If you can't decide whether a phrase is a simile or a metaphor, it helps to just refer to it as an example of imagery.

The first person ('I')

It is perfectly appropriate to say 'I feel' or 'I think' to express your opinion. Just remember that you are being asked for your opinion about **what** Dickens may have been trying to convey in his novel (his themes and ideas) and **how** he does this (through characters, events, language, form and structure of the novel).

Spelling, punctuation and grammar (AO4)

Spelling, punctuation and grammar are specifically targeted for assessment on the nineteenth-century novel only by OCR. However, even for other exam boards you cannot afford to forget that you will demonstrate your grasp of the novel through the way you write – so take great care with this and don't be sloppy. If the examiner cannot understand what you are trying to say, they will not be able to give you credit for it.

How to raise your grade

The most important advice is to answer the question that is in front of you, and that you need to start doing this straight away. When writing essays in other subjects, you may have been taught to write a lengthy, elegant introduction explaining what you are about to do. You have only a short time in the Literature examination so it's best to get cracking as soon as you've gathered your thoughts together and made a brief plan.

Sometimes students go into panic mode because they don't know how to start. It is absolutely fine to begin your response with the words, 'In this extract Dickens presents…', if you are answering an extract-based question for any of the exam boards.

Begin by picking out interesting words and phrases and unpicking or exploring them within the context or focus of the question. For example, if the question is about the way that poverty is presented, you need to focus on picking out words and phrases to do with poverty.

What methods has the writer used? Although there is a whole range of methods with which you need to be familiar, it might be something as simple as a powerful adjective. What do you think is the impact of that word? It might be that the word you are referring to has more than one meaning. If that's the case, the examiner will be impressed if you can discuss what the word means to you, but can also suggest other meanings. Is context relevant here? In other words, would Dickens' readers have viewed poverty differently from a modern reader? What might Dickens have been trying to express about poverty when he chose this word or phrase?

> **GRADE BOOSTER**
>
> It is important to make the individual quotations that you select brief and to try to **embed** them. This will save you time, enabling you to develop your points at greater depth and so raise your grade.

It is likely that you will find it easier to address AO2 (methods) when writing about the extract as you have the actual words to hand.

Is there an actual overall effect? For instance, you may have noticed Dickens' frequent use of lists of adjectives that create intensely vivid impressions, so as well as analysing individual words in the list (not necessarily all of them – just the most interesting ones) you could also describe the cumulative effect.

Be very careful to avoid lapsing into narrative (retelling the story). If you are asked about how Dickens presents Pip, remember that the focus of the question is about the methods that Dickens uses (*how* he presents the character). Do not simply tell the examiner what Pip does or what he is like; this is a very common mistake.

Remember you also have to deal with the focus of the question in the novel as a whole, or in the case of Edexcel and OCR 'elsewhere in the novel'. You will be penalised if you do not do this so you **must** leave time. If you feel you have more to offer in terms of comments on the extract, leave a space so that you can come back and expand on this if you have time.

Key points to remember

- Do not just jump straight in! Spending time wisely in the first moments may gain you extra marks later.
- Write a brief plan.
- Remember to answer the question.
- Refer closely to *details* in the passage in your answer, support your comments, and remember that you must also refer to the novel as a whole (or to 'elsewhere' in the novel for Edexcel and OCR).
- Use your time wisely! Try to leave a few minutes to look back over your work and check your spelling, punctuation and grammar, to ensure your meaning is clear and so that you know that you have done the very best that you can.
- Keep an eye on the clock!

GRADE *FOCUS*

Grade 5
- Candidates have a clear focus on the text and the task and are able to 'read between the lines'.
- Candidates develop a clear understanding of the ways in which writers use language, form and structure to create effects for the reader.
- Candidates use a range of detailed textual evidence to support their comments.
- Candidates use understanding of the idea that both writers and readers may be influenced by where, when and why a text is produced.

GRADE *FOCUS*

Grade 8

- Candidates produce a consistently convincing, informed response to a range of meanings and ideas within the text.
- Candidates use ideas that are well linked and that often build on one another.
- Candidates dig deep into the text, examining, exploring and evaluating writers' use of language, form and structure.
- Candidates carefully select finely judged textual references that are well integrated in order to support and develop responses to texts.
- Candidates show perceptive understanding of how contexts shape texts and responses to texts.

Aiming for a Grade 9

To reach the very highest level you need to have thought about the novel more deeply and to have produced a response that is conceptualised, critical and exploratory at a deeper level. You might, for instance, challenge accepted critical views in evaluating whether the writer has always been successful. If, for example, you think Dickens set out to create sympathy for the poor, how successful do you think he has been?

You need to make original points clearly and succinctly and to convince the examiner that your viewpoint is really your own, and a valid one, with constant and careful reference to the text. This will be aided by the use of short and apposite (meaning really relevant) quotations, skilfully embedded in your answer along the way (see 'Sample essays' on p.79).

REVIEW YOUR LEARNING

(Answers are given on p.101.)

1 Can you take your copy of the novel into the exam?
2 Why is it important to read the whole question carefully before you do anything else?
3 Why is it important to plan your answer?
4 Why is it important to keep an eye on the clock?
5 Will you be assessed on spelling, punctuation and grammar in your response to *Great Expectations*?
6 What should you do if you finish ahead of time?

Assessment Objectives and skills

All GCSE examinations are pinned to specific areas of learning that the examiners want to be sure the candidates have mastered. These are known as Assessment Objectives or AOs. If you are studying *Great Expectations* as an examination text for AQA, Edexcel or OCR, the examiner marking your exam response will be trying to give you marks, using the particular mark scheme for that board. All mark schemes, however, are based on fulfilling the key AOs for English literature.

Assessment Objectives

The Assessment Objectives that apply to your response to *Great Expectations* are given below.

For AQA, Edexcel and OCR:

AO1 Read, understand and respond to texts. Students should be able to:
- maintain a critical style and develop an informed personal response
- use textual references, including quotations, to support and illustrate interpretations.

AO2 Analyse the language, form and structure used by a writer to create meanings and effects, using relevant subject terminology where appropriate.

For AQA and OCR only:

AO3 Show understanding of the relationship between texts and the contexts in which they were written.

If you are entered for the Edexcel examination, AO3 is not assessed on the *Great Expectations* question.

For OCR only:

AO4 Use a range of vocabulary and sentence structures for clarity, purpose and effect, with accurate spelling and punctuation.

You can't forget about AO4 entirely even if it is not applicable to your exam board for this text, as it will probably be assessed on another part of the paper (usually Section A). That being said, if your spelling or punctuation leaves something to be desired, you can lift your spirits by reminding yourself that AO4 is worth only about 5 per cent of your total mark!

What skills do you need to show?

Let's break the Assessment Objectives down to see what they really mean.

> **AO1** Read, understand and respond to texts. Students should be able to:
> - maintain a critical style and develop an informed personal response
> - use textual references, including quotations, to support and illustrate interpretations.

At its most basic level, this AO is about having a good grasp of what a text is about and being able to express an opinion about it within the context of the question. For example, if you were to say, 'The novel is about a naïve boy called Pip', you would be beginning to address AO1 because you have made a '**personal**' response. An '**informed**' response refers to the basis on which you make that judgement. In other words, you need to show that you know the novel well enough to answer the question.

The AO also requires you to '**use textual references, including quotations, to support and illustrate interpretations**'. This means giving short direct quotations from the text. For example, if you wanted to support the idea that Pip is hopelessly infatuated with Estella, you could use a direct quote: 'I ... said to my pillow, "I love her, I love her, I love her!" hundreds of times'. Alternatively, you can simply refer to details in the text in order to support your views. So you might say, 'Pip's obsession with Estella is indicated by his repeated declarations of love for her while lying restlessly in bed.'

Generally speaking, most candidates find AO1 relatively easy. Usually, it is tackled well – if you answer the question you are asked, this Assessment Objective will probably take care of itself.

> **AO2** Analyse the language, form and structure used by a writer to create meanings and effects, using relevant subject terminology where appropriate.

AO2 is a different matter. Most examiners would probably agree that covering AO2 is a weakness for many candidates, particularly those students who only ever talk about characters as if they were real people.

In simple terms, AO2 refers to the writer's methods and is often signposted in questions by the word 'how' or by the phrase 'How does the writer present...'.

Overall, AO2 is equal in importance to AO1 so it is vital that you are fully aware of this objective. The word '**language**' refers to Dickens' use of words. Remember that writers choose words very carefully in order to achieve particular effects. They may spend quite a long time deciding between two or three words with similar meanings in order to create just the precise effect that they are looking for.

When you are addressing AO2 in your response to *Great Expectations*, you will typically find yourself using Dickens' name and exploring the choices he has made. For example, 'Dickens has Pip refer to Miss Havisham as "waxwork" and "skeleton"' will set you on the right path to explaining why these words are an interesting choice. Of course, there is no right or wrong answer, but you might say that the words suggest, firstly, lifelessness and, secondly, death, thus dehumanising Miss Havisham and so emphasising the extent of her physical and psychological deterioration. Both are images of potential horror to a child and thus Dickens also uses these words to better enable the reader to see how disturbing a figure Miss Havisham is from the young Pip's point of view.

Language encompasses a wide range of writer's methods, such as the use of different types of imagery, words that create sound effects, litotes, irony and so on. AO2 also refers to your use of '**subject terminology**'. This means that you should be able to use terms such as 'metaphor', 'alliteration' and 'hyperbole' with confidence and understanding. Don't despair, however, if you can't remember the term – you will still gain marks for explaining the effects being created!

The terms '**form**' and '**structure**' refer to the kind of text you are studying and how it has been 'put together' by the writer. This might include the narrative technique being used (in *Great Expectations* Dickens uses the first-person narrator); the genre(s) the text is part of; the order of events and the effects created by this; and the way key events are juxtaposed. For example, the description of the freezing cold and intimidating graveyard in Chapter 1 in which Magwitch unexpectedly surprises Pip contrasts powerfully with the 'chimney corner' at which the comforting Joe sits in Chapter 2. Effects of structure can also be seen in the writer's use of sentence lengths and word order (syntax).

Remember – if you do not address AO2 at all, it will be very difficult to achieve much higher than Grade 1, since you will not be answering the question.

> **AO3** Show understanding of the relationship between texts and the contexts in which they were written.

This AO, although not perhaps considered as important as AO1 and AO2, is still worth between 15 and 20 per cent of your total mark for the examination as a whole, and so its importance should not be underestimated. Do remember, however, that it is not assessed for this novel if you are entered with Edexcel.

To cover AO3, you must show that you understand the links between a text and when, why and for whom it was written. For example, some awareness of the class structure in Victorian England may well help you to understand Dickens' intentions in writing *Great Expectations* – that is, to help change the attitudes of a largely middle-class readership with regard to how those in the upper classes should behave. Equally, some knowledge of Dickens' background might give you useful insight into his concern about the treatment of children in the nineteenth century.

It is important, however, to understand that context should not be 'bolted on' to your response for no good reason; you are writing about literature not history!

> **AO4** Use a range of vocabulary and sentence structures for clarity, purpose and effect, with accurate spelling and punctuation.

This AO is fairly self-explanatory. It is worth remembering that it is assessed in your response to *Great Expectations* only by OCR. A clear and well-written response, however, should always be your aim: if your spelling is so bad or your grammar and lack of punctuation so confusing that the examiner cannot understand what you are trying to express, this will obviously adversely affect your mark!

Similarly, although there are no marks awarded for good handwriting, and none taken away for untidiness or crossings outs, it is vital for the examiner to be able to read what you have written. If you believe your handwriting is so illegible that it may cause difficulties, speak to your school's examination officer in plenty of time before the exam. They may be able to arrange for you to have a scribe or to sit your examination using a computer.

What you will not gain many marks for

You will not gain many marks if you do the following:

- **Retell the story.** You can be sure that the examiner marking your response knows the story inside out. A key feature of the lowest grades is 'retelling the story'. Don't do it.
- **Quote long passages.** Remember, the point is that every reference and piece of quotation must serve a very specific point you are making. If you quote at length, the examiner will have to guess which bit of the quotation you mean to serve your point. Don't impose work on the examiner – be explicit about exactly which words you have found specific meaning in. Keep quotes short and smart.

- **Merely identify literary devices.** You will never gain marks simply for identifying literary devices, such as use of a simile or a rhyme. You can gain marks, however, by identifying these features, exploring the reasons why you think the author has used them and offering a thoughtful consideration of how they might impact on readers, as well as giving an evaluation of how effective you think they are.
- **Give unsubstantiated opinions.** The examiner will be keen to give you marks for your opinions, but only if they are supported by reasoned argument and references to the text.
- **Write about characters as if they are real people.** It is important to remember that characters are constructs – the writer is responsible for what the characters do and say. Don't ignore the author!

REVIEW YOUR LEARNING

(Answers are given on p.102.)

1 What is AO1 assessing?
2 What is AO2 assessing?
3 What is AO3 assessing?
4 What is AO4 assessing?
5 Which two of the Assessment Objectives are most important?
6 What should you avoid doing in your responses?

Sample essays

Target your thinking

- What type of question will you face on your GCSE English literature examination?
- What are examiners looking for when they assess your work?
- What are the features of Grade 8 and Grade 5 answers?
- What does a well-structured essay look like?
- What is the most effective way to use quotations and textual references?

Below, you will find a Grade 8 response and a Grade 5 response to an extract-based character question and to an extract-based thematic question. All four responses have been fully annotated with examiners' comments so that you can see how the grades awarded relate to the four Assessment Objectives for GCSE English literature. In other words, you will be able to see exactly how to write a top grade answer, and you will gain an insight into exactly what examiners are looking for when they award one of the above grades.

Question 1: character-based

Read the following passage from Chapter 38 and then answer the question below. (Extract taken from pages 304–05 of the Penguin Classics edition.)

Starting with this extract, write about how Dickens presents the balance of power in the relationship between Estella and Miss Havisham.

Write about:

- how Dickens presents Estella's thoughts and feelings in this extract
- how Dickens presents the balance of power in the relationship between Estella and Miss Havisham in the novel as a whole.

[30 marks]

"Mother by adoption," retorted Estella, never departing from the easy grace of her attitude, never raising her voice as the other did, never yielding either to anger or tenderness, "Mother by adoption, I have said that I owe everything to you. All I possess is freely yours. All that you have given me, is at your command to have again. Beyond that, I have nothing. And if you ask me to give you what you never gave me, my gratitude and duty cannot do impossibilities."

"Did I never give her love!" cried Miss Havisham, turning wildly to me. "Did I never give her a burning love, inseparable from jealousy at all times, and from sharp pain, while she speaks thus to me! Let her call me mad, let her call me mad!"

"Why should I call you mad," returned Estella, "I, of all people? Does anyone live, who knows what set purposes you have, half as well as I do? Does anyone live, who knows what a steady memory you have, half as well as I do? I who have sat on this same hearth on the little stool that is even now beside you there, learning your lessons and looking up into your face, when your face was strange and frightened me!"

"Soon forgotten!" moaned Miss Havisham. "Times soon forgotten!"

"No, not forgotten," retorted Estella. "Not forgotten, but treasured up in my memory. When have you found me false to your teaching? When have you found me unmindful of your lessons? When have you found me giving admission here," she touched her bosom with her hand, "to anything that you excluded? Be just to me."

"So proud, so proud!" moaned Miss Havisham, pushing away her grey hair with both her hands.

"Who taught me to be proud?" returned Estella. "Who praised me when I learnt my lesson?"

"So hard, so hard!" moaned Miss Havisham, with her former action.

"Who taught me to be hard?" returned Estella. "Who praised me when I learnt my lesson?"

"But to be proud and hard to *me*!" Miss Havisham quite shrieked, as she stretched out her arms. "Estella, Estella, Estella, to be proud and hard to *me*!"

Estella looked at her for a moment with a kind of calm wonder, but was not otherwise disturbed; when the moment was past, she looked down at the fire again.

Grade 8 sample answer

A01: The candidate demonstrates a most astute understanding of Estella's personality and of how her development into an adult has changed the nature of the relationship between the two.

The most striking aspect in the evolution of the balance of power in the relationship between these two characters at this point in the novel arises out of the maturity and detachment that Estella now displays, very different from the early scenes between her and Miss Havisham when Estella was quite simply a spoilt, precocious and dependent child. One way in which Dickens presents this maturity and detachment is through his choice of Estella's language, which remains admirably restrained despite the preposterous nature of Miss Havisham's demands for love:

A01 and A02: Excellent foregrounding of the author, displaying an astute awareness that the characters are literary creations and not real people; very close attention paid to the exact wording of the question; excellent use of quotation shortened with ellipsis as evidence.

"All I possess is freely yours … And if you ask me to give you what you never gave me, my gratitude, and duty cannot do impossibilities."

Of course, as she never received love as a child, the ability to love is not one of Estella's 'possessions'. Admittedly, love would be a normal expectation of a mother from a child that she has raised but it is Miss Havisham's motivation for adopting Estella – revenge rather than love – which makes her sudden requirement for demonstrable affection unreasonable. Significantly, Dickens has Estella refer to 'gratitude' and 'duty', thus highlighting that Estella is bound to Miss Havisham by dispassionate obligation rather by than by affection.

A01 and A02: Excellent explanation of how the evidence proves the point that the candidate is making about Dickens' use of language to reveal Estella's attitude to Miss Havisham.

A01 and A02: The candidate has successfully explored a second way in which Dickens reveals Estella's character – through her behaviour in this scene. Again, the candidate has developed the point with appropriate evidence and compelling analysis.

Similarly, not only is Estella's language restrained but so is her behaviour, again indicating a mature disposition and a consequent shift in the balance of power. Dickens has Pip describe 'the easy grace of her attitude', which Dickens then deliberately contrasts sharply with the moaning and the outraged outbursts of Miss Havisham.

A01: The candidate has successfully developed a third sophisticated and original point regarding the way in which Dickens reveals Estella's character. This time, the candidate has provided evidence in the form of a highly accurate paraphrase rather than through direct quotation of what Estella says to Miss Havisham in defence of her lack of affection.

The contrast in behaviour between the two further serves to emphasise Estella's composure and general superiority.

Dickens also has Estella respond to Miss Havisham's childlike demands for love with reasoned argument, again a most adult quality. She is effectively able to counter all of Miss Havisham's unfair accusations with shrewd psychological analysis. As Estella explains, if she appears unaffectionate, this is not as a result of ingratitude but as a result of an inability to encompass such an emotion. And, as she calmly rationalises, the fault is not her own, but Miss Havisham's. It is the mentor who taught the child to be aloof and unaffectionate. Estella's inability to connect emotionally is not a sign of immaturity or ingratitude — but of damage.

One of Dickens' main uses of language to indicate the balance of power between the two women is his choice of speech tags to describe the verbal responses that take place between them during the dialogue in this scene. He deliberately repeats the word 'moaned' to indicate the strength of Miss Havisham's injured feelings. He also uses the words 'cried' and 'shrieked'. For Estella, however, he repeatedly uses the word 'returned', which suggests that she is more engaged in a logical disputation and, hence, more in control. This further emphasises her lack of emotional engagement and her inability to empathise with Miss Havisham's distress. The phrase 'Estella looked at her for a moment with a kind of calm wonder' also revealingly betrays Estella's lack of empathy, especially Dickens' careful choice of the word 'wonder'.

A02: Excellent analysis of Dickens' use of language and, again, a most relevant and perceptive approach to the question.

A01: As in the whole essay, the candidate supports the point being made by following the evidence with a most astute analysis.

A02: This is analysis of the author's use of language at the highest level.

Another striking use of language to reveal Estella's attitude towards Miss Havisham is the phrase 'Mother by adoption'. It quite clearly characterises their relationship as a legal contract rather than an emotional bond.

AO1: As always, this candidate is rigorously focused on the question.

The passage clearly depicts Miss Havisham's distress at Estella's inability to respond to her supposed maternal love. One way in which Dickens signals this distress is by having her repeatedly push back her hair. The phrase 'shrieked, as she stretched out her arms' is an even more powerful physical sign of Miss Havisham's anguish and, hence, relative weakness. It is also very noticeable that Estella does not respond to these gestures and, instead, looks into the fire. This may well be symbolic as writers often use fire to represent passion, and passion is exactly what Estella is incapable of feeling.

AO2: Another excellent analysis of Dickens' use of language to communicate subtler and more symbolic layers of meaning to the reader.

AO1: The candidate continues to impress and is now setting about analysing the power balance in this relationship in 'the novel as a whole'.

It is in Chapter 8 when Dickens first introduces these two characters. At this point, Estella is merely a child and Miss Havisham is her guardian and so the power balance between the two is quite different:

'Your own, one day, my dear, and you will use it well. Let me see you play cards with this boy!' (p.60)

AO2: Excellent understanding displayed of the potential symbolism here.

The first statement in the above quotation refers to an expensive jewel which Miss Havisham has held against Estella's bosom and hair … almost as if Estella were a doll or a plaything. Clearly, Dickens is establishing from the outset that Estella is regarded by her mentor as little more than an extension of Miss Havisham's will. The jewel is also being used as a bribe and so it is evident that the nature of their relationship has always been transactional. As we have already seen from the analysis of the above extract, this monetary dimension to their relationship will come back to haunt Miss Havisham towards the end of her life. Of course, the corrupting power of money is one of the accusations that Dickens frequently levels against Victorian society…

AO3: This is the first of a number of connections that the candidate makes between events in the novel and the wider social context.

AO1: Another excellent choice of scene and the candidate clearly is demonstrating a most relevant knowledge of 'the novel as whole'.

AO4 (assessed by OCR only on this type of question): This is an exceptionally well written and precise response that uses a sophisticated range of sentence structures and vocabulary. Spelling, punctuation and grammar are exceptionally accurate.

Dickens reintroduces Estella in Volume 2 after she returns from her schooling abroad. As far as Miss Havisham is concerned, Estella is still nothing more than an instrument of revenge and it is clear that Estella is still very much under Miss Havisham's control. As she declares to Pip: 'We are not free to follow our own devices, you and I' (Chapter 33, p.265). Here, Dickens may not only be alluding to the darker workings of his own carefully crafted plot, but also to Victorian society in general, as children then were not afforded the degree of independence and protection that we teenagers often take for granted today.

AO3: Again, the candidate astutely seizes the opportunity to relate the novel to its social context and so continues to gain credit for this important Assessment Objective.

This is an extremely well-focused analysis that thoroughly addresses all of the Assessment Objectives and explores how Dickens uses a wide variety of literary devices in order to develop the dynamic relationship between the two characters. As the complete version of this essay shows, an excellent balance has been maintained between both bullet points in the question, i.e. the initial analysis of the extract and the consequent exploration of this relationship at various key moments in the novel. The introduction is clear and concise and the conclusion (not included here) is powerful and most effectively summarises Estella's ultimate triumph in her struggle to be free of Miss Havisham's corrupting influence. The response does everything to achieve a Grade 8, and shows signs of going even higher.

Grade 5 sample answer

AO1: The candidate has correctly identified one possible aspect of Estella's personality and has developed the point using textual reference and analysis of that reference reasonably effectively. The candidate is relying solely on Miss Havisham's opinion of Estella in order to justify this point, however, instead of considering Dickens' overall presentation of Estella. Miss Havisham's opinion of Estella is unlikely to be reliable as she is a misguided character and in a great deal of distress.

AO1 and AO2: This is a better-developed point but it would have been even more powerful had the candidate referred to Dickens' skill here and made it clear that the ambiguity belongs to Dickens and not to Miss Havisham.

AO4: As one would expect at Grade 5, the overall communication is clear but some of the sentences can be rather awkwardly constructed at times.

Estella comes over as quite an arrogant person in the passage: 'So proud, so proud!' moaned Miss Havisham. The fact that she says it twice is more evidence of Estella's pride. Estella also seems to be a person who is incapable of love and this is powerfully indicated by her use of the term 'Mother by adoption' when addressing Miss Havisham. It is not the way that a child would refer to a parent that was loved.

It suggests that Miss Havisham has a power over Estella which is based on the authority that an adult would automatically have over a child in a society that was as unsympathetic to children as Victorian society was. Because of his own treatment as a child, Dickens was very sensitive to this sort of thing. But Miss Havisham is deeply disappointed that Estella is unable to offer anything more.

Miss Havisham obviously loves Estella as a daughter but Estella is distant and cold towards her and this is why Miss Havisham becomes distressed. Even when Miss Havisham stretches out her arms and shows desperation for affection, Estella still does not show her any love. Miss Havisham's repeated outburst of 'Let her call me mad!' is clever because the ambiguity expresses both her anger and her delicate sanity as a result of her great anguish at Estella's lack of love for her. As Estella is more in control of herself, she appears to be the much stronger person.

Miss Havisham is obviously extremely annoyed with Estella because of the lack of love that she is receiving from her. When she repeatedly accuses Estella of being 'proud' and 'hard', she shows how upset she is as you would not use such emotive vocabulary to someone who you felt

The candidate has a tendency to regard the characters as real people rather than as constructs created by the author.

AO1 and AO3: This is a good point but the candidate could have deepened it by explaining why Estella is unable to show affection. After all, Dickens has included Estella's more reliable explanation for her lack of feeling in the passage. The reference to the Victorian attitude towards children is insightful but not particularly developed.

AO2: A good observation regarding the use of repetition and a good use of the word 'emotive' to describe such vocabulary but, again, the candidate has failed to acknowledge that these vocabulary choices belong to Dickens and not to his fictional creation.

A01: The candidate appears to be in danger of losing sight of the fact that this first part of the question is actually asking for the focus to be primarily upon Estella and not on Miss Havisham.

A03: An appropriate and relevant historical reference to the relationship between the novel and its social context.

A01: The candidate makes an intelligent link between this section of the novel and the passage that featured in the first part of the question.

A01: The candidate is really beginning to show depth of insight here, and Dickens as author is being consistently acknowledged. To be pedantic, though, Estella is a character and not a real woman.

really loved you back. Because she has to demand love from Estella, it makes Estella appear to be the stronger person. Miss Havisham also uses a lot of exclamation marks to show how upset she is: 'So proud, so proud!' moaned Miss Havisham.

Chapter 8 is the first time when the reader is introduced to both Estella and Miss Havisham. Miss Havisham is still the same control freak as we see later in the novel but Dickens' first presentation of Estella shows a different character in the sense that she is a child and so far more under Miss Havisham's power, and this reveals to the modern reader the authority that a parent had over a child during this period.

One of the first descriptions of Estella is that 'her light came along the long dark passage like a star' (p.59). In this metaphor, Dickens is symbolically suggesting that Estella is well beyond Pip's reach and that his love for her is doomed to failure. The image also suggests that Estella is beautiful but cold and lacking in affection which is, of course, an aspect of her character that has not changed in the adult Estella that we see Miss Havisham complaining about in the passage above.

When Estella announces that she is going to marry Drummle, Dickens is showing a really big change in her relationship with Miss Havisham because she is finally breaking free of her adopted mother's financial control. Dickens shows Miss Havisham's shock to the reader when Pip says that Miss Havisham puts her hand to her heart. However, Estella is now an extremely damaged young woman and that might be why she is seeking out such an abusive husband. This is really deep, especially when you consider when Dickens was writing.

A01: The use of the term 'control freak' is perceptive, if a little inappropriate as examiners tend to reward more formal and precise vocabulary. It is heart-warming, however, to see the candidate finally, and very convincingly, demonstrating an awareness of Dickens' role as author!

A02: The candidate analyses Dickens' use of the image well, although he/she does make the common error of confusing a simile with a metaphor. A further problem is that this analysis of language is not sufficiently related to the question. The quotation appears to have been included simply because it has been memorised!

A03: Indeed! As the candidate suggests, this does seem to be a very modern psychological insight. The candidate could have related this very good point to the question much more, however, i.e. the proposed marriage to Drummle is evidence that, psychologically, Estella is still suffering from Miss Havisham's corrosive influence.

A04 (assessed by OCR only): The range and quality of sentence structures and vocabulary is always competent and, sometimes, quite sophisticated. Meaning is clearly conveyed and spelling, punctuation and grammar are very accurate.

The sophistication and depth of thought is less consistent than one would expect to find in a higher-scoring candidate, but the essay is generally well focused on the question. There has been a mostly successful attempt to support the points being made via apt textual reference and some very pertinent analysis. The second part of the essay is more convincing than the first part as it demonstrates more awareness of Dickens' role as author and this is the deciding factor in awarding this a Grade 5.

Question 2: thematic

Read the following passage from Chapter 4 and then answer the question below. (Extract taken from pages 25–26 of the Penguin Classics edition.)

Starting with this extract, write about how Dickens presents attitudes towards children.

Write about:

- how Dickens presents the attitude of the adults towards children in this extract
- how Dickens presents attitudes towards children in the novel as a whole.

[30 marks]

Among this good company I should have felt myself, even if I hadn't robbed the pantry, in a false position. Not because I was squeezed in at an acute angle of the table-cloth, with the table in my chest, and the Pumblechookian elbow in my eye, nor because I was not allowed to speak (I didn't want to speak), nor because I was regaled with the scaly tips of the drumsticks of the fowls, and with those obscure corners of pork of which the pig, when living, had had the least reason to be vain. No; I should not have minded that, if they would only have left me alone. But they wouldn't leave me alone. They seemed to think the opportunity lost, if they failed to point the conversation at me, every now and then, and stick the point into me. I might have been an unfortunate little bull in a Spanish arena, I got so smartingly touched up by these moral goads.

It began the moment we sat down to dinner. Mr. Wopsle said grace with theatrical declamation – as it now appears to me, something like a religious cross of the Ghost in Hamlet with Richard the Third – and ended with the very proper aspiration that we might be truly grateful. Upon which my sister fixed me with her eye, and said, in a low reproachful voice, "Do you hear that? Be grateful."

> "Especially," said Mr. Pumblechook, "be grateful, boy, to them which brought you up by hand."
>
> Mrs. Hubble shook her head, and contemplating me with a mournful presentiment that I should come to no good, asked, "Why is it that the young are never grateful?" This moral mystery seemed too much for the company until Mr. Hubble tersely solved it by saying, "Naterally wicious." Everybody then murmured "True!" and looked at me in a particularly unpleasant and personal manner.

Grade 8 sample answer

AO1: The candidate has clearly read the question carefully, realising that focus should be on attitudes towards children in general, thus resisting the temptation to respond to the passage solely in terms of Pip's treatment.

In this scene, Dickens presents the disregard of Victorian adults towards the wellbeing of children via the combined spite of all of the adults which is aimed at the only child present, Pip. As the adult behaviour is so vindictive, the reader's sympathy is automatically aroused for Pip who proves himself to be a gentle soul well capable of suffering in silence.

One of the ways that Dickens morally undermines and condemns the behaviour of the adults towards Pip is by setting the scene on Christmas Day. Their unpleasant 'moral goads' about Pip's ingratitude for the extremely poor quality of meal that he is experiencing, i.e. the 'obscure corners of pork', contrast sharply with the Christian celebration. Throughout the novel, Dickens frequently upholds the virtues of humility and self-sacrifice in order to expose the hypocrisy of both his characters and his society.

AO3: The candidate displays an excellent understanding of the importance of morality in Dickens' writing.

Obviously, it is the adult Pip who, as narrator, is recollecting and then relating the events of this day, as Dickens makes explicit through the comment 'as it now appears to me...' and by the reference to the two Shakespeare plays. This is what enables Dickens to allow Pip the use of such sophisticated humour and language.

AO2: An excellent knowledge of Dickens' narrative style is displayed here. And Dickens himself is clearly foregrounded!

AO2: A most perceptive analysis of various aspects of Dickens' use of language in order to create sympathy for Pip.

For example, Dickens has the narrator refer to being 'an unfortunate little bull in a Spanish arena.' The use of the word 'little' reminds the reader that Pip is just a very young child and hence vulnerable. The word 'arena' also conjures up images of both spectacle and cruelty, as in a Roman gladiatorial arena. But Dickens also cleverly combines this with the authentic voice of a child in mental discomfort: 'they wouldn't leave me alone.'

As well as imagery, Dickens also satirises and ridicules the adults by the manner in which he presents their speech, for example Mr Hubble's remark that the young in general are 'Naterally wicious.' The phonetic spelling clearly exposes Hubble's poor pronunciation, which is obviously Dickens' way of suggesting to his reader that Hubble's opinion concerning the corrupted nature of youth is based on ignorance and prejudice and, therefore, of no value. Certainly, when contrasted with the perfect Standard English of Pip's unspoken observations, Hubble seems very inferior in both expression and thought. And the fact that Pip has no voice apart from the inner voice of his thoughts perfectly exemplifies the Victorian belief that children were to be seen but not heard.

Interestingly, Dickens has rather masked the full unpleasantness of the situation by his use of the mocking narrative tone, exaggerated humour, caricature and eloquent imagery. In this way, Dickens almost obscures the true unpleasantness of Pip's childhood. Pumblechook's reference to being grateful to 'them which brought you up by hand' is clearly an example of Dickens' irony, the darker allusion being to Mrs Joe's use of 'Tickler', her cane.

AO3: Another very insightful comment, in which the candidate demonstrates a clear understanding of the relationship between the text and the social context in which it was written.

AO2: This time, the candidate focuses on even more aspects of Dickens' use of language to sway the sympathies of the reader towards Pip.

AO1: The point is clearly related to the question and is highly insightful. There is use of both relevant short quotation and succinct paraphrase as evidence to support the point. The analysis of evidence is extremely perceptive, yet concise.

AO3: Here, the candidate most effectively signals the second part of the essay while simultaneously outlining a major contrast in Dickens' presentation of the theme. →

A much more serious presentation of the self-seeking and insensitive attitude of adults towards children in Victorian society is that of Miss Havisham's corruption of Estella's childhood, which results in long-term psychological damage as Miss Havisham determines to dehumanise Estella and turn her into little more than a mean-spirited, and ultimately miserable, instrument of her own revenge against men.

The candidate then continues to address the theme effectively as it is developed in 'the novel as a whole'. The student's concluding paragraph is below.

AO3: A brilliant conclusion in which the candidate makes a number of extremely skilful references to context in terms of our society, Victorian society and Dickens' own personal history. →

Perhaps the intensity with which Dickens explores this theme of frequent maltreatment towards children is as a result of his own personal experiences, especially the great distress he must have felt when separated from his family at a young age and forced to work in the boot blacking factory. This overwhelming sense of powerlessness may well be why Dickens presents both Pip and Estella as child victims who lack any form of protection. Even the otherwise virtuous Joe is not allowed to stand between Pip and the ferocity of Mrs Joe. In many respects, the novel can be read as a manifesto for greater awareness of both physical and psychological abuse towards children. In this respect, it is as relevant today as it was when Dickens wrote it!

AO4 (assessed by OCR only): This is an exceptionally well written and precise essay, which uses a sophisticated range of sentence structures and vocabulary. Spelling, punctuation and grammar are exceptionally accurate.

As one would expect with a candidate scoring at Grade 8, the quality of insight is extremely sophisticated and mature and is well supported by a range of pertinent references and an impressive depth of analysis of Dickens' use of language, style and structure, as well as providing a number of excellent comments regarding the relationship between the novel and its social background. This response is extremely well structured and highly focused on the question. It does everything to achieve a Grade 8, and shows signs of going even higher.

Grade 5 sample answer

AO1: The candidate launches in without explicitly referencing the question.

AO3: There is an attempt here to relate the novel to its social context and the observation made is valid, if somewhat simplistic. It is also a relief to see that the candidate is finally addressing the wider context of the question, i.e. attitudes to children, and not just the treatment of Pip.

AO2: Finally, a reference to Dickens and authorial intent! It's also good to see technical terms such as 'imagery' being used. The quotation could have been integrated into the paragraph, however.

> Even though it is Christmas Day, the adults in the scene are obviously unkind to Pip and so when he refers to 'this good company' he is clearly being sarcastic. Pip is visibly not enjoying the meal because he begins with a long list of complaints, including the fact that he has to sit at a corner of the table and the fact that he has Pumblechook's elbow in his eye. When Pip describes himself as having the 'table in my chest' it helps to create sympathy for him because it makes him appear very small. Also the fact that he was 'squeezed in' suggests that he wasn't really wanted there and that they are just putting up with him because it is Christmas Day. In Victorian times, children were often treated as second class citizens whereas today they are well protected by law.
>
> Dickens also uses imagery in order to show how badly Pip is being treated:
>
> 'I might have been an unfortunate little bull in a Spanish arena, I got so smartingly touched up by these moral goads.'
>
> In Spain, bulls were killed by matadors during bull fights and so Pip must feel as if he is in danger. Or, at least, he is feeling very uncomfortable with these adults. The use of the word 'smartingly' is clever as when you get an injury, it can 'smart' or hurt. Perhaps he is worried that he will be hit? Certainly, Mrs Joe does use Tickler a lot.

AO1 and AO2: The candidate is providing observations that are clearly related to the Assessment Objectives. The analysis of Dickens' use of language is perceptive as it does display an awareness of deeper nuances beyond the literal meaning. Unfortunately, the candidate is missing opportunities to foreground Dickens by continually writing as if Pip himself is the author rather than just a creation.

AO1 and AO2: Again, an effective point and the analysis of the possible impact of Dickens' use of the word 'smartingly' is unexpectedly astute.

The candidate then continues to address the theme in 'the novel as a whole' reasonably effectively. The candidate's concluding paragraph has been included below.

AO1: While everything that the candidate says is accurate, the conclusion merely summarises what he/she has already said and so is a wasted opportunity as it adds nothing new for the examiner to credit.

> Thus Dickens presents children as victims throughout his novel. As I said at the start of this essay, Pip is a victim during the Christmas dinner. He is also a victim when he visits Miss Havisham and he is often badly mistreated by his sister, Mrs Joe. Estella is a victim because she is psychologically abused by Miss Havisham and so grows up to be an abuser herself. Dickens also shows neglect of children's needs in general through the poor quality of schooling that the local children receive at the school where Biddy helps out.

AO4 (assessed by OCR only): The range and sophistication of sentence structures and vocabulary is competent, and meaning is clearly conveyed. Some technical vocabulary has been correctly used. Spelling, punctuation and grammar are very accurate.

The candidate makes a number of good points, which are reasonably well developed with apt textual reference and some valid analyses. The response is generally well focused upon the question, although the deeper implications of Dickens' craft as author and the implied point in the question about Pip exemplifying the theme of attitudes towards children in general have been only partially addressed. There has been a good attempt at examining the effects of language and there is accurate use of some pertinent subject terminology. The second part of the essay, where the candidate responds to the bullet point regarding 'the novel as a whole', does address attitudes to children more directly and Dickens' role as author is frequently acknowledged. Altogether, there is enough to justify the essay being awarded a Grade 5.

Top quotations

As your examination will be 'closed book', and you will only have a short extract in front of you, you might find it helpful to memorise some quotations to use in support of your points in the examination response.

Top characterisation quotations

Pip

'I wanted to make Joe less ignorant and common, that he might be worthier of my society and less open to Estella's reproach.' (Chapter 15, p.109)

1

- Pip's infatuation with Estella has corrupted his natural and innocent affection for Joe and replaced it with such shallow conventional values as snobbery and a reverence for social status.

'The beautiful young lady at Miss Havisham's, and she's more beautiful than anybody ever was, and I admire her dreadfully, and I want to be a gentleman on her account.' (Chapter 17, p.129)

2

- An explicit linkage between Pip's misguided social aspiration and his obsession with Estella.

'...my sense of my own worthless conduct to them was greater than every consideration.' (Chapter 39, p.323)

3

- Having learned the base origin of his 'great expectations' (that being Magwitch) Pip finally comes to his senses and rediscovers his own innate morality.

'...I lay there, penitently whispering, "O God bless him! O god bless this gentle Christian man!"' (Chapter 57, p.463)

4

- Pip reconnects with Joe and with his Christian faith, putting spiritual truths before material concerns, thus achieving moral redemption.

Estella

1 'I have no softness there, no – sympathy – sentiment – nonsense.' (Chapter 29, p.237)

- Miss Havisham has so corrupted Estella that she has made her incapable of compassion, love and empathy.

2 'And if you ask me to give you what you never gave me, my gratitude and duty cannot do impossibilities.' (Chapter 38, p.304–05)

- A powerful irony, and the moment when Miss Havisham realises, much to her horror, that the instrument of revenge that she has created cannot give her the filial affection that she now craves.

3 '...I am tired of the life I have led, which has very few charms for me, and I am willing enough to change it.' (Chapter 44, p.364)

- In order to escape the futility of her own existence as Miss Havisham's instrument of revenge, the psychologically damaged Estella enters into a self-destructive marriage with Drummle.

4 '...suffering has been stronger than all other teaching, and has taught me to understand what your heart used to be. I have been bent and broken, but – I hope – into a better shape.' (Chapter 59, p.484)

- Like Pip, Estella finds moral redemption through great sorrow and so eventually learns to appreciate such fine human qualities as love and compassion.

Miss Havisham

1 '...she had the appearance of having dropped, body and soul, within and without, under the weight of a crushing blow.' (Chapter 8, p.61)

- When considering Miss Havisham's cruel and spiteful behaviour, especially towards Pip, it is important to remember that she is herself a victim suffering from a terrible grief.

2 'If she favours you, love her. If she wounds you, love her. If she tears your heart to pieces – and as it gets older and stronger, it will tear deeper – love her, love her, love her!' (Chapter 29, p.240)

- A good example of Miss Havisham at her most malicious.

'...until I saw in you a looking-glass that showed me what I once felt myself, I did not know what I had done.' (Chapter 49, p.399)

3

- As with Pip and Estella, Miss Havisham also comes to learn the error of her ways, here finally discovering empathy and compassion.

'...I stole her heart away and put ice in its place.' (Chapter 49, p.399)

4

- A stark image, which most powerfully portrays how Miss Havisham deliberately corrupted and damaged Estella for her own twisted revenge.

Magwitch

'If I ain't a gentleman, nor yet ain't got no learning, I'm the owner of such.' (Chapter 39, p.321)

1

- Rather like Miss Havisham and Estella, Magwitch becomes Pip's benefactor in order to further his own agenda, that being to defy the society that victimised and criminalised him.

'In jail and out of jail, in jail and out of jail...' (Chapter 42, p.346)

2

- A very tragic and succinct summary of Magwitch's life prior to his transportation to Australia.

'I must put something into my stomach, mustn't I?' (Chapter 42, p.347)

3

- A deceptively simple quotation that explains that poverty and deprivation were the root causes of Magwitch's criminality.

'...he had taken to industrious habits, and had thriven lawfully and reputably.' (Chapter 56, p.456)

4

- Having been allowed the opportunity to better himself when in Australia, Magwitch became a model citizen.

Joe

'He was a mild, good-natured, sweet-tempered, easy-going, foolish, dear fellow...' (Chapter 2, p.8)

1

- Via Pip's narration, Dickens delivers a very succinct and self-explanatory summary of Joe's virtuous nature, if somewhat limited intelligence.

2 '...a sort of Hercules in strength, and also in weakness. (Chapter 2, p.8)
- Another succinct and telling summary. Although a physically powerful man, Joe is very timid.

3 '...I'm dead afeerd of going wrong in the way of not doing what's right by a woman...' (Chapter 7, pp.49–50)
- This reveals why Joe tolerates Mrs Joe's unreasonable behaviour, because he wants to avoid being the tyrant that his father had been to his mother.

4 'If you can't get to be oncommon through going straight, you'll never get to do it through going crooked.' (Chapter 9, p.72)
- Despite his limited learning and intelligence, Joe has a natural wisdom, which Dickens wants the reader to admire and respect.

Top moments in the novel

1 'I thought I overheard Miss Havisham answer – only it seemed so unlikely – "Well? You can break his heart."' (Chapter 8, p.60)
- This creates powerful plot interest via dramatic foreshadowing and is the first time in the novel that Dickens reveals how Miss Havisham will use Estella as a weapon against the male sex.

2 '...I thought long after I laid me down, how common Estella would consider Joe, a mere blacksmith: how thick his boots, and how coarse his hands.' (Chapter 9, p.72)
- This reveals Dickens' dismay at the shallow, superficial and indolent nature of many in the upper classes and also shows how corrupting such notions of class can be.

3 'Biddy,' I exclaimed, impatiently, 'I am not at all happy as I am. I am disgusted with my calling and with my life.' (Chapter 17, pp.127–28)
- This highlights Pip's dissatisfaction with his situation in life as Joe's apprentice, and emphasises how social aspiration, especially if based on snobbery, makes one lose sight of fundamental values such as love, obligation, loyalty and gratitude.

'That girl's hard and haughty and capricious to the last degree, and has been brought up by Miss Havisham to wreak revenge on all the male sex.' (Chapter 22, p.177)

4

- Herbert's warning to Pip creates a great deal of suspense via dramatic foreshadowing and provides an invaluable insight into two of the main characters, Estella and Miss Havisham.

Herbert, quoting his father, tells Pip: '...no man who was not a true gentleman at heart, ever was, since the world began, a true gentleman in manner.' (Chapter 22, p.181)

5

- Dickens uses Herbert as a mouthpiece in order make the important moral point regarding the way in which a gentleman should behave, i.e. with honesty and integrity.

'We spent as much money as we could, and got as little for it as people could make up their minds to give us. We were always more or less miserable...' (Chapter 34, p.274)

6

- Dickens is severely criticising the empty, shallow, self-indulgent and unproductive lives that far too many privileged people led during his time.

'...blast you every one, from the judge in his wig, to the colonist a stirring up the dust, I'll show a better gentleman than the whole kit on you put together!' (Chapter 40, p.332)

7

- Pip is not a real gentleman but one manufactured by an ex-convict (Magwitch) and thus has no real social status. Furthermore, Pip's social elevation, like Estella's, is based on another's desire for revenge.

'"O Miss Havisham," said I, "I can do it now. There have been sore mistakes; and my life has been a blind and thankless one; and I want forgiveness and direction far too much, to be bitter with you."' (Chapter 49, p.398)

8

- This displays Pip's enormous moral growth, which takes place towards the end of the novel once his pretentions to gentility have been undermined by Magwitch's revelations.

9 'I went towards them slowly, for my limbs were weak, but with a sense of increasing relief as I drew nearer to them, and a sense of leaving arrogance and untruthfulness further and further behind.' (Chapter 58, p.477)

- Here Dickens reveals the psychological wellbeing that can be derived from living a moral existence as opposed to the shallow 'genteel' attributes of snobbery, deceit and self-interest.

10 '...I saw the shadow of no parting from her.' (Chapter 59, p.484)

- The closing line of the novel, in which Dickens provides the long-anticipated happy ending to satisfy the reader.

Top thematic quotations

Crime and punishment

1 'While I looked about me here, an exceedingly dirty and partially drunk minister of justice asked me if I would like to step in and hear a trial or so...' (Chapter 20, p.165)

- The legal system is clearly presented here as corrupt and debased.

2 As Magwitch explains to Pip, 'when I was a ragged little creetur as much to be pitied as ever I see ... I got the name of being hardened.' (Chapter 42, p.346)

- Unfortunately, Victorian society made no allowances for crime caused by poverty.

3 'And when we're sentenced, ain't it him as gets seven year, and me fourteen, and ain't it him as the Judge is sorry for...' (Chapter 42, p.351)

- Dickens highlights how unequal the justice system is.

Children

1 'In the little world in which children have their existence whosoever brings them up, there is nothing so finely perceived and so finely felt, as injustice.' (Chapter 8, p.63)

- Dickens constantly raises concerns about the vulnerability of children in his novels.

'...for, we think the feelings that are very serious in a man quite comical in a boy...' (Chapter 15, p.115)

2

- This very telling quotation reveals the lack of empathy for children in Victorian society.

'Put the case that he lived in an atmosphere of evil, and that all he saw of children, was, their being generated in great numbers for certain destruction.' (Chapter 51, p.413)

3

- Dickens, via Jaggers, laments the loss of so many children who end up criminalised through adverse circumstance and then harshly prosecuted by the courts.

Morality and belief

'...those noble passages were read which remind humanity how it brought nothing into the world and can take nothing out...' (Chapter 35, p.281)

1

- This reference to the Bible reminds the reader of the dangers of being overwhelmed by materialism and so of losing sight of the spiritual dimension beyond earthly existence.

'...passing on, with absolute equality, to the greater Judgement that knoweth all things and cannot err.' (Chapter 56, p.458)

2

- A reminder to Dickens' readers of God's judgement after death on how a person conducted his or her life.

Money and materialism

'I thought Mr. Jaggers glanced at Joe, as if he considered him a fool for his disinterestedness.' (Chapter 18, pp.137–38)

1

- Joe refuses to take financial compensation for the loss of Pip because he loves him but Dickens, via Pip, implies that such natural affection is peculiar in such a materialistic society.

'So, Mr. Trabb measured and calculated me ... as if I were an estate...' (Chapter 19, p.152)

2

- Dickens highlights how having wealth sometimes makes a person more valued as a result of the materialistic nature of Victorian society.

Answers

Answers to the *Review your learning* questions.

Context (p.14)

1 1812–70.

2 Pip's home town is based on Rochester.

3 1822.

4 Charles Dickens' father was imprisoned for debt and Charles Dickens had to work in a boot-blacking factory.

5 Dickens had a love affair with Ellen Ternan.

6 He is stressing the importance of moral behaviour through Pip's progress and through the fact that Pip's 'saviours', Magwitch and Joe, are both men whose humanity and virtues are strong. Consequently, they are characters who the reader can really admire.

Plot and structure (p.30)

1 1807.

2 Seven.

3 Fourteen or fifteen.

4 'Suspense' means creating questions in the reader's mind that can be answered only by reading on.

5 To prevent the reader from becoming bored or frustrated.

6 They delay the main action and, therefore, the answers to the big areas of suspense.

7 The Gothic.

8 Through the comments of other characters.

Characterisation (p.43)

1 A character's actions; a character's dialogue and what other people say about that character; a character's thoughts; the narrator's observations about a character; imagery.

2 'Charactonym' is the technique of giving characters names that reflect their personality and/or appearance.

3 All of them.

4 As a child he is naïve and innocent. After he comes into his 'great expectations', he becomes elitist and egocentric. After he discovers whom his real benefactor is, he starts to care about other people again.

5   Miss Havisham is a victim of Compeyson's cruel betrayal of her on her wedding day. Estella is a victim of Miss Havisham's desire for revenge.

6   Magwitch represents both the essential nobility of the common man and the morally corrupting influence of poverty and deprivation.

Themes (p.53)

1   Gentility and social class; education; justice and mercy; romantic love; forgiveness and redemption.

2   Victorian society can be seen as unjust, class-ridden and materialistic.

3   All of them!

4   Social class, education and romantic love.

5   Miss Havisham.

6   Joe, because of the way in which Pip snobbishly rejected him.

7   Miss Havisham, Mrs Joe and Arthur.

8   Sympathetic.

Language, style and analysis (p.64)

1   A writer's style comprises the distinctive characteristics of their work that help to make that writer unique.

2   There are two narrative voices – the ironic voice of Dickens and the more romantic voice of Pip.

3   Places are often used symbolically.

4   Some of the techniques that Dickens uses in order to create humour include slapstick comedy, exaggeration, ludicrous behaviour and speech, irony, juxtaposition, incongruity, imagery and puns.

5   Mrs Joe and Pumblechook are not treated seriously. This is because they are neither morally virtuous like Biddy nor tragically flawed like Miss Havisham and Estella.

6   Because Orlick's violence is meant to be frightening and not humorous.

7   Figurative language is the use of literary devices such as metaphor, simile and personification.

8   A motif is a recurring image or idea.

Tackling the examination questions (p.73)

1   No, as it is a 'closed book' examination.

2   In order to make sure that you fully understand the question.

3   In order to ensure that your answer is relevant and fully focused.

4   In order to ensure that you give equal time to all parts of the question.

5   Only if you are entered for OCR.

6   Check your work for obvious SPaG errors and in order to make sure that it makes good sense.

Assessment Objectives and skills (p.78)

1   Your overall grasp of what the text is about; your ability to express an interpretation of it within the context of the question; your ability to support and develop that interpretation with appropriate textual reference.

2   Your ability to analyse the language, form and structure used by a writer to create meanings and effects, using relevant subject terminology where appropriate.

3   Your ability to show an understanding of the relationships between texts and the contexts in which they were written.

4   The effectiveness and sophistication of your vocabulary and sentence structures and the accuracy of your spelling, punctuation and grammar.

5   AO1 and AO2.

6   Simply retelling the story; quoting long passages; identifying techniques used by an author without explaining the possible intended effects of these techniques on the reader; giving unsubstantiated opinions (opinions not backed up by evidence); writing about the characters as if they are real people.

Wider reading

- The Penguin Classics edition of *Great Expectations* (ISBN: 978-0-141-43956-3). This contains a most useful introduction to the novel, a chronological list of the main events in Dickens' life, and explanatory notes that explain the meaning or significance of many of the references in the text. Furthermore, all page numbers in this guide relate to this edition of the novel.

- **www.gutenberg.org/files/1400/1400-h/1400-h.htm** – the Project Gutenberg ebook of *Great Expectations*. Using the search function on your browser, you can type in key words and quickly search for such things as particular passages or imagery patterns.

- **http://charlesdickenspage.com/expectations.html** by David Perdue – a potted summary of the entire plot and brief descriptions of the characters.

- **www.shmoop.com/great-expectations** – extremely detailed (and most amusingly written) summaries of every chapter in the novel.

- **http://en.wikipedia.org/wiki/Great_Expectations** – extremely detailed information about both the novel and the context.

- **www.bbc.co.uk/schools/gcsebitesize/english_literature/ prosegreatexpect** – the BBC's brief study guide to the novel.

- **www.bl.uk/romantics-and-victorians/articles/the-gothic-in-great-expectations** by Professor John Bowen – an insightful essay about the influence of the Gothic tradition on *Great Expectations*.

- **www.nybooks.com/articles/archives/2010/jun/10/who-was-charles-dickens** by Robert Gottlieb – a most interesting review of both Dickens' life and his work.

- **www.bbc.co.uk/history/historic_figures/dickens_charles.shtml** – the BBC's brief biography of Charles Dickens.

- **www.bbc.co.uk/schools/primaryhistory/victorian_britain** – the BBC's useful resource for those wishing to understand more about life in Victorian Britain.

- **www.victorian-era.org/victorian-era-society.html** – an explanation of the class structure in Victorian Britain.

- **www.victorianweb.org/history/gentleman.html** by David Cody – a detailed explanation of what being a gentleman meant in Victorian Britain.

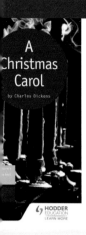